UNITED WE STAND, DIVIDED WE FALL:
OPPOSING TRUMP'S AGENDA

ESSAYS ON PROTEST AND RESISTANCE AND
WHAT WE CAN DO TO STOP HIM

UNITED WE STAND, DIVIDED WE FALL: OPPOSING TRUMP'S AGENDA

ESSAYS ON PROTEST AND RESISTANCE AND WHAT WE CAN DO TO STOP HIM

DENNY TAYLOR

YOHURU WILLIAMS

JONATHAN FOLEY

CHARLENE SMITH

DAVID JOSEPH KOLB

P.L. THOMAS

JENNIFER BERKSHIRE

MORNA MCDERMOTT

STEVEN SINGER

RUSS WALSH

KATIE LAPHAM

ANNE HAAS DYSON

ESTHER SOKOLOV FINE

VANESSA BARNETT

CAROLYN WALKER

STEVE NELSON

GEORGE LAKOFF

GARN PRESS
NEW YORK, NY

Published by Garn Press, LLC
New York, NY
www.garnpress.com

Book and cover design by Benjamin J. Taylor/Garn Press

First Edition, March 2017

Library of Congress Control Number: 2017903116

Publisher's Cataloging-in-Publication Data

Names: Taylor, Denny. | Williams, Yohuru. | Foley, Jonathan. | Smith, Charlene. | Kolb, David Joseph. | Thomas, P. L. | Berkshire, Jennifer. | McDermott, Morna. | Singer, Steven. | Walsh, Russ. | Lapham, Katie. | Dyson, Anne Haas. | Fine, Esther Sokolov. | Vanessa Barnett. | Walker, Carolyn. | Nelson, Steve. | Lakoff, George.
Title: United we stand divided we fall : resisting trump's agenda – essays on protest and resistance and what we can do to stop him / Denny Taylor, et al.
Description: First edition. | New York : Garn Press, 2017. | Includes bibliographical references.
Identifiers: LCCN 2017903116 | ISBN 978-1-942146-57-5 (pbk.) | ISBN 978-1-942146-58-2 (Kindle ebook)
Subjects: LCSH: Civil disobedience. | Civil rights. | Fascism. | Government, Resistance to. | Racism. | Mass media and propaganda. | BISAC: POLITICAL SCIENCE / Corruption & Misconduct. | POLITICAL SCIENCE / Propaganda. | POLITICAL SCIENCE / Political Ideologies / Democracy. | POLITICAL SCIENCE / Political Ideologies / Fascism & Totalitarianism. | POLITICAL SCIENCE / Political Process / Media & Internet. | SOCIAL SCIENCE / Discrimination & Race Relations).
Classification: LCC JC328.3 .T487 2017 (print) | LCC JC328.3 (ebook) | DDC 323.73--dc23.
LC record available at https://lccn.loc.gov/2017903116.

CONTENTS

INTRODUCTION

DENNY TAYLOR

In *United We Stand Divided We Fall* Garn Press has gathered together essays by great scientists, scholars and renowned teachers who oppose the direction in which President Trump is leading the country. These are essays, to quote George Lakoff, which frame American values accurately and systemically day after day, telling truths by American majority moral values.

These are essays of protest against and resistance to Trump's presidency, to his billionaire cabinet, to the privileging in the White House of white supremacists, the promulgation of "alternate facts", the denigration of media sources, the purges of State Department personnel, the gag orders at the EPA and scientists placed on "watch lists", the travel bans on people from wide swaths of U.S. society and on refugees ... the list is long.

They are also essays that tackle the question of what we can do to stop Trump from becoming a fast moving catastrophe. When the hands of the Doomsday Clock were moved closer to midnight, President Trump was named specifically as an existential risk to humanity. There is no doubt that we must all act. The writers of conscience who have written this collection of essays are all actively engaged in opposing President Trump and their writings encourage us to participate in the resistance movement. Read with a pencil in hand. Make notes on what you can do to join aspects of the movement that reflects the needs and concerns of your community. Through social media you can go global while acting locally.

Keep in mind as your read and write in the margins of the book that you are actively engaged in responding to the very particular ways in which the writers and those they write about see the world. As James Baldwin said in his debate with William Buckley at the University of Cambridge in 1965, our response to questions that are "hideously loaded" depend in effect on "where you find yourself in the world, what your sense of reality is, what your *system* of reality is. That is, it depends on assumptions, which we hold so deeply so as to be scarcely aware of them."

Stepping into this arena to engage the public in ways that might, quite possibly, shine a light on assumptions that have been hidden or camouflaged for many years are the scientists, scholars and teachers who have contributed to *United We Stand, Divided We Fall: Opposing Trump's Agenda – Essays on Protest and Resistance:*

Yohuru Williams: Yohuru R. Williams is Professor of History and Author of *Black Politics/White Power: Civil Rights Black Power and Black Panthers in New Haven*

Denny Taylor: Denny Taylor is Professor Emeritus of Literacy Studies, Novelist, Children's Author, and Founder of Garn Press

Jonathan Foley: Jonathan Foley is a World-Leading Environmental Scientist and Executive Director of the California Academy of Sciences

Charlene Smith: Charlene Smith is a Journalist, Documentary Film Maker, Author and Biographer of President Nelson Mandela

David Joseph Kolb: David Joseph Kolb is a Prize Winning Reporter, Editor and Columnist, and Author of *Devil Knows: Tale of Murder and Madness in America's First Century* (Garn Press)

P.L. Thomas: P.L. Thomas is a Recipient of the NCTE George Orwell Award and Author of *Beware the Roadbuilders* and *Trumplandia* (Garn Press)

Jennifer C. Berkshire: Jennifer Berkshire is a Writer, Editor, and Author of the *Have You Heard* Blog and Co-Host of its Weekly Podcast on "Education in the Time of Trump"

Morna McDermott: Morna McDermott is Professor of Education and Co-Editor of *Testing Our Courage: United Opt Out and the Testing Resistance Movement*

Steven Singer: Steven Singer is a Public School Teacher, Education Advocate and Author of the *Gadfly on the Wall* Blog

Russ Walsh: Russ Walsh is a Public School Teacher, Literacy Specialist, Curriculum Supervisor and College Instructor, and Author of *A Parent's Guide to Public Education* (Garn Press) and the *Russ on Reading* Blog

Katie Lapham: Katie Lapham is a NYC Public School Teacher and Author of the *Critical Classrooms, Critical Kids* Blog

Anne Haas Dyson: Anne Haas Dyson is Professor of Education, a Recipient of the NCTE Outstanding Educator of the Year Award, and Author of *Negotiating a Permeable Curriculum* (Garn Press)

Esther Sokolov Fine: Esther Sokolov Fine is Professor Emerita of Education, Former Elementary School Teacher in Downtown Public Housing Communities and Alternative Programs, and Author of *Raising Peacemakers* (Garn Press)

Vanessa Barnett: Vanessa Barnett is School District Arts Program Coordinator, University Arts Instructor, and Museum Arts Consultant

Carolyn Walker: Carolyn Walker is a journalist, memoirist, essayist, poet, and creative writing instructor nominated for a Pushcart Prize, and Author of *Every Least Sparrow* (Garn Press)

Steve Nelson: Steve Nelson, Head of Calhoun School 1998-2017 in NYC, one of America's most notable progressive schools, and Author of *First Do No Harm: Progressive Education in a Time of Existential Risk* (Garn Press)

George Lakoff: George Lakoff, Professor Emeritus of Cognitive Science and Linguistics, is a World Renowned Linguist Integrating Studies of Social Issues and Politics from a Neural Linguistics Perspective

THE PRINCIPLES FOR WHICH WE FIGHT

YOHURU WILLIAMS

Yohuru R. Williams is Professor of History and Author of "Black Politics/White Power: Civil Rights Black Power and Black Panthers in New Haven"

"Is this for real?" a friend texted me the day after the 2016 election. "Is Donald Trump really the president? What can we do?" Even now, almost four months removed from the contest, I can't remember how I responded but I will never forget the feeling. For scores of people both in the United States and across the globe, it was a destabilizing moment wrought with fear and uncertainty. Complicated by electoral calculus, it was at once both like and different from the contested election of 2000 in which Al Gore won the popular vote but George Bush won in the Electoral College. Like many others, I was disappointed in the outcome. Few questioned the fitness of the president-elect to serve. At the time, there were no sustained demonstrations in the streets catalyzed by the candidate's campaign rhetoric of hate and division, no shadowy ties with Russia suggesting a stolen election, and no hastily fashioned Muslim ban solidifying the clear and present danger posed by a leader uninformed by constitutional practice as well as democratic principle.

It was a moment further complicated by the erosion of trust in some of the most important safeguards of American democracy including the media and public schools; both came under assault in the early days of the Trump Administration. Every time I open my Internet browser or turn on the news I am reminded of the advice proffered at the opening of Roald Dahl's, *Twilight Zone* inspired television series *Tales of the Unexpected.* "A wise man," the narrator cautioned with each show, "only believes in lies, trusts in the absurd, and learns to expect the unexpected." We now live in a time when facts no longer matter and lies become matter of fact. This is our new realty ensured by the personality and style of the man at the center of this political maelstrom.

It would perhaps be easier to tolerate if there were something remotely presidential about Trump, but his whole biography, not to mention his rhetoric and behavior on the campaign trail contribute to the profound sense that he is not. It was easy early on to scoff at the cartoonish exaggerations of the man known as "The Donald" who also brought us *The Art of the Deal*, the failed XFL and the reality show *The Apprentice*. We also have to acknowledge that before he claimed the Republican nomination Trump's antics were at least somewhat amusing. He turned the Republican political debates into a reality show that while distressing was hard to turn off.

New Jersey Star Ledger editorial cartoonist Drew Sheneman perhaps expressed it best after a particularly embarrassing, if entertaining, Trump debate performance, in July of 2015. "A year from now we'll look back at the past week as the instance the wheels started to come off the Trump express." He forecast, "Running down war heroes and handing out senatorial cell phone numbers is just the beginning. Donald Trump will eventually implode and if the past few weeks are any indication, it will be in spectacular fashion." Admitting that he had not been closely following the Republican debates, Sheneman, nevertheless announced his intention to continue to "tune in to watch Trump and his cotton-candy clown, low grade-school caliber insults at other prospective leaders of the free world." It was outrageous with just enough danger to compel our attention like passengers on a roller coaster or adolescent visitors to a haunted house where speed and darkness blunt the impulse to flee out of the relative security we feel in spite of the carefully curated illusions, climbs and dips, with men in masks to assist our suspension of disbelief.

But the implosion that Sheneman and scores of others predicted never materialized. Now nearly a year and half later we all find ourselves uncomfortably suspended in the dark and disquieting confines of the ride with only a faint notion of how long it will actually last. The former freak show having lost its entertainment value primarily because the implosion that still seems inevitable – given the cavalcade of scandals and foreign intrigue – could have a devastating impact both at home and abroad.

In the United States, the damage has been most acute to our core American values, those fundamental beliefs that inform our civil theology and have been the hallmark of what it means to be an American. In its clear assault and repudiation of the essence of these values, Trumpism has placed our democracy in real jeopardy. Ironically in his inaugural address, Trump sought to channel those principles and values in a stirring rhetoric fundamentally at odds with reality of his proposed agenda. He recommended for instance that, "We must speak our minds openly, debate our disagreements honestly, but always pursue solidarity". Yet his relationship with the media and political opponents has been a study in deception and suppression.

Trump's address also articulated conflicting foreign policy goals that at once pledged restraint and at the same time committed the US to leadership in a worldwide campaign against "Islamic" Terrorism. As he explained, "We do not seek to impose our way of life on anyone, but rather to let it shine as an example for everyone to follow." He continued, "We will reinforce old alliances and form new ones – and unite the civilized world against Radical Islamic Terrorism, which we will eradicate completely from the face of the Earth."

It seems inconceivable that neither Trump nor his speech-writers appreciated the problematic nature of this dictum with its troubling claim of uniting the "civilized world" in what would amount to a war against Islam. If the speech left nothing to the imagination, the administration's ill-conceived Muslim Travel Ban that followed shortly thereafter left little to doubt.

In this case and so many others, Trumpism represents an abandonment of the most basic principles of truth, fairness, and equality so eloquently expressed by countless Americans from Thomas Jefferson to Alice Paul and Martin Luther King, Jr. over the course of the history of the Republic. The constellation of ideas expressed in the foundational documents of this nation and consecrated not only by the blood of those who served in foreign wars, but also by those who have been martyred for the extension, advocacy, and preservation of American democracy at home. This includes not only the stalwart women and men who led the campaign to abolish slavery but the dedicated activists who worked to secure women's suffrage and civil rights. Often forgotten, it also includes efforts to insure the fair and equitable treatment of immigrants from a wide spectrum of people seeking economic opportunity to those in search of political asylum. Those seeking pathways to ensure the preservation of American core values at this time act in the best tradition of such freedom fighters.

What exactly informs our values? The National Council for the Social Studies produced a useful chart1 for elementary students that present them in a clear and concise fashion, part of our continuing effort to becoming what the founders called "a more perfect union." They include a respect for Life, Liberty, and the Pursuit of Happiness but much more, including Truth.

In the "era" of Trump the insistence on "Truth", the idea that "the government and citizens should not lie" may prove the most significant. It is a call to action rooted in our need to speak truth to power in an effort to preserve the ideals that have been essential to our tradition of open and transparent government and freedom of speech. At a time when conversations about "Alt News" and "Alt Facts" have penetrated the national debate and the head of state has denounced the free press, it is not only the insistence on but also the search for truth that should guide our work and our activism. Likewise, we should reject a definition of Patriotism predicated on the crude jingoism of a bygone era. Instead we should embrace what the council powerfully describes as a "devotion to our country and the core democratic values in word and deed."

The entire list is reproduced below. They are transparent enough for everyone to understand, share and succinctly restate. They are also convenient benchmarks for measuring the ways in which Trumpism betrayed them. Most importantly, these are principles around which we must organize and fight.

Life: Each citizen has the right to the protection of his or her life.

Liberty: Liberty includes the freedom to believe what you want, freedom to choose your own friends, and to have your own ideas and opinions, to express your ideas in public, the right for people to meet in groups, the right to have any lawful job or business.

The Pursuit of Happiness: Each citizen can find happiness in their own way, so long as they do not step on the rights of others.

Justice: All people should be treated fairly in getting advantages and disadvantages of our country. No group or person should be favored.

Common Good: Citizens should work together for the good of all. The government should make laws that are good for everyone.

Equality: Everyone should get the same treatment regardless of where their parents or grandparents were born, race, religion or how much money you have. Citizens all have political, social and economic equality.

Truth: The government and citizens should not lie.

Diversity: Differences in language, dress, food, where parents or grandparents were born, race, and religion are not only allowed but accepted as important.

Popular Sovereignty: The power of the government comes from the people.

Patriotism: A devotion to our country and the core democratic values in word and deed.

LOVE TRUMPS HATE: THE DESCENT OF DONALD TRUMP INTO THE AMERICAN PSYCHE AND THE DISSENT OF THE PEOPLE

DENNY TAYLOR

Denny Taylor is Professor Emeritus of Literacy Studies, Novelist, Children's Author, and Founder of Garn Press

"Love Trumps Hate!" a crowd of many thousands at an anti-Trump rally shouted on Central Park West outside the Trump Hotel at Columbus Circle on Sunday, November 13, 2016.

This anti-Trump demonstration followed the protest march on Saturday, November 12, which had begun in Union Square and moved north on Broadway to Trump Tower, the 58-story home of Donald Trump.

"Not my president!" the angry crowd shouted in unison on Saturday as they reached the police barricades across Fifth Avenue one block from Trump Tower and forced the marchers to loop over to Sixth Avenue and back crowding the block in front of the Tower and the blocks between West 55ᵗʰ and 57ᵗʰ street.

The signs at both protests were graphic: Trump Racist Fascist Misogynist; Fight the Billionaire; Dump Trump; Respect Existence or Expect Resistance; Aqui Estamos Nos Vamos (Here to stay); I protest for the Black Lives taken from us and for the Muslim lives that are threatened."

But the atmosphere at the Sunday anti-Trump rally was more peaceful. "Yesterday was good for our souls," a teacher said who had participated in the Saturday protest.

"We won't stop," a woman said, on Sunday at Columbus Circle. She was holding up a sign on which was written, "No Trump, No KKK, No Fascists." The woman had brought her young daughter and niece to the demonstration and they were holding up the signs they had made. Her daughter had written "Trump Trump Go Way Racist Sexist Anti Gay", and her niece had written "When We Stand United Hate Can't Divide Us".

Her young daughter was leading many of the shout-outs including "Hey! Hey! Ho! Ho! Donald Trump has got to go!"

Her daughter tried a new shout out, "We can't live like this ..."

"Not catchy enough," her mother said laughing.

"Boycott Trump!" her daughter shouted and people around her began to shout with her.

"We'll keep it up for four years if we have to," her mother said, "but he'll be gone before then"

She might be right. It is a long time since so many Americans have taken to the streets and there have been only a few occasions when they have done so with such determination and fervor and each time they triumphed. The suffragettes succeeded and women got the vote, Civil Rights activists succeeded and segregation was outlawed and African Americans got the vote, and when anti-war protesters took to the streets across the United States the Vietnam War ended.

It can be done. The people have the power when they coalesce. The protesters, rich and poor, of every hue it is possible for a human being to be, of different ethnicities and religions, old and young, little children and babies, immigrants and citizens alike were standing together in solidarity. Together they embodied the idea that "Love Trumps Hate." It was not just a group of angry people holding up signs shouting. They were joking and laughing with one another acting out the sign, "Make America Love Again."

On the edge of the crowd at the entrance to Central Park three neatly dressed young men, tall and white, were standing watching the people participating in the anti-Trump demonstration. One of the young men was crying and his two companions had aghast looks on their faces as they surveyed the vast crowd of people who were so peacefully standing with their anti-hate signs protesting against Trump becoming the 45th President of the United States.

The young man who was crying said something to his companions and with angry looks on their faces they turned away. But the crown did not notice, they were shouting in unison – "The people united will never be defeated!"

Few would argue that Trump has brought out the best and the worst in America. He has exposed both the nation's capacity to love and to hate. He has put the vulnerable and all those who care for and about them on notice that they are not safe, and he has created a space for white hate groups, many members of armed militias, to move out of the shadows into mainstream society – which they have done committing vile acts of hate.

The Southern Poverty Law Center[2] reported 200 incidents of hate crimes between November 9 and 11. Anti-Black and Anti-immigrant incidents were far and away the most reported with anti-Muslim being the third most common.

Examples of the Trump related hateful harassment and intimidation that occurred in the first three days following the presidential election are included on the SPLC website including:

My 12 year old daughter is African American. A boy approached her and said, "now that Trump is president, I'm going to shoot you and all the blacks I can find"

"Death to Diversity" was written on a banner displayed on our library for people to see, as well as written on posters across campus. As well as white males going up to women saying that it was now "legal to grab them by the pussy".

I was standing at a red light waiting to cross the street. A black truck with three white men pulled up to the red light. One of them yelled, "Fuck your black life!" The other two began to laugh. One began to chant "Trump!" as they drove away.

The KKK has endorsed Trump with SPLC reprinting the Tweet by David Duke in which he states, "Our people played a HUGE role in electing Trump!"

While the extreme right in the U.S. and U.K. (Nigel Farage) support Trump, so do poor older white women who have had hard lives and believe Trump when he says he will Make American Great Again (MAGA). It's an odd combination – men with

Swastika tattoos and grandmothers in pink and yellow cardigans make excuses for his sewer of a mouth and, say it's just the way he talks. "He doesn't mean it," they say. But anything is possible if you are making it all up and don't have a moral base on which your participation in society is grounded. You can say one thing and then other, appeal to this group and then to that group, and gather people susceptible to that kind of talk around you.

It is a different kind of vulnerability than being of color, a woman, or immigrant. Many people in human societies are vulnerable to indoctrination and mass psychology. In the mid 1930's an English teacher was in Germany and attended a Hitler youth rally at which he heard Hitler say, "We want you to be peace-loving and strong."

And the English teacher said he felt himself getting caught up in the moment, the energy, the excitement, the noble ideal, and he raised his arm with the youth attending the rally and shouted "Heil Hitler!" with them.

Hitler wrote in Mein Kampf:

… all effective propaganda must be limited to a very few points and must harp on these in slogans until the last member of the public understands what you want him to understand by your slogan.

… No matter what amount of talent is employed in the organisation of propaganda, it will have no result if due account is not taken of these fundamental principles. Propaganda must be limited to a few simple themes and these must be represented again and again. Here, as in innumerable other cases, perseverance is the first and most important condition of success

… Only constant repetition will finally succeed in imprint-

ing an idea on the memory of the crowd.

Trump used Hitler's technique just as effectively as Hitler did. Here is Trump and some of his recurring messages that he repeated over and over throughout the presidential campaign:

I will make America first, again. America first!

Our country is going bad. We're going to save our country.

We cannot be so politically correct anymore.

It's unfair what's happened to the people of our country and we're going to fix it.

I will outline reforms to add millions of new jobs,

I will restore law and order to our country. The crime and violence ... will soon, and I mean very soon, will come to an end.

We are going to build a great border wall to stop illegal immigration, to stop the gangs and the violence, and to stop the drugs from pouring into our communities.

These themes and were repeated at every rally, and Trump built his base using the same fundamental principles of propaganda Hitler outlined in *Mein Kampf*. There are disturbing similarities – as well as differences – between Germany in the 1930's and the United States in the second decade of the 21st century, but here we will stick to the susceptibility of some people in society to the propaganda that Hitler used and Trump is now using to secure his base.

Trump supporters defend Trump and can be heard in TV and radio interviews saying:

Donald Trump has pulled off a miracle.

I think I know him. He loves America.

He's not a racist.

He's not a bigot.

Special interests on the left are setting him up for their short-term interests.

He did say incredible vociferous things and people took him seriously – I did not.

Let's not pretend. I was against him, but I think Trump will re-imagine American society.

Anyone who sees the negative side of him is not being truthful.

The greatest danger confronting the people in the United States and around the world is their exorable desire to normalize Trump's behavior. Again there are parallels with the British Parliament and Neville Chamberlain's blinding desire to normalize the behavior of Adolf Hitler. "This morning I had another talk with the German Chancellor, Herr Hitler," Chamberlain announced when he landed at Heston Airport on September 30, 1938, "and here is the paper which bears his name upon it as well as mine…. We regard the agreement signed last night and the Anglo-German Naval Agreement, as symbolic of the desire of our two peoples never to go to war with one another again." [3]

Eleven months later on September 3, 1939, Chamberlain broadcast from the Cabinet Rooms at 10 Downing Street,[4] "It is evil things that we will be fighting against – brute force, bad faith, injustice, oppression and persecution – and against them I am certain that the right will prevail."

The desire for normality is a phenomenon that we are experiencing today.

Rationalization and even victimization is exemplified by one woman's struggle to find a way forward in her thinking about Trump. "He's a deeply wounded man," she said, "and respect could heal him."

Don't be fooled.

Across the country thousands of people are volunteering to accompany people targeted by Trump – immigrants, Muslims, African Americans to work each day because of the sharp rise in harassment and hate crimes.

Here's the message from Morris Dees, Founder, Southern Poverty Law Center:

> Like you, I'm very concerned about the future of our nation. I never imagined that the election of a new president would result in Nazi swastikas being spray-painted on businesses and middle school students being bullied with chants of "build the wall."

Just since Election Day, SPLC has:

- Exposed Trump's transition team members' extremist links

- Provided teachers with free resources to help them heal the scars the campaign left on students

- Alerted the country to white supremacists' reaction to Trump's victory

- Begun tracking incidents of racist harassment linked to Trump's accession

- Launched a petition telling Donald Trump to publicly reject hatred and bigotry

P.S. Please set an example in your community. Speak out against hate and bigotry whenever and wherever you see it.

Simon Schama in *FT Weekend* November 12/13, 2016 [5] argues that this is not a moment to "calm down." He writes:

Bowing to the judgment of the polls does not entail a suspension of dissent, especially, when, as in this case, the election involves shameless suppression of votes, the politicization of the FBI and the cyber-interference of the Russians.

Schama lays out what is on the line: the repeal of the Affordable Care Act depriving 25 million Americans of insurance; the overthrow of the Roe v Wade ruling on abortion; the repudiation of the Paris Climate Agreement; the abandonment of the Iran nuclear agreement, and so much more.

He concludes:

Whatever rises from the rubble of liberalism's debacle must never repeat that mistake. The decencies of modern life need to be argued with militant passion and broadcast to places where it can be heard by people who don't read broadsheets. What neither America not the rest of the world can afford right now is to keep calm and carry on.

Still, maintaining the importance of the peaceful transition of power, President Obama did say in a Special News Conference on Monday November 15, that Trump had "executed one of the biggest political upsets in history." Obama spoke of "folks missing the Trump phenomenon" adding "I don't think he is ideological."

One reporter asks him if he has concerns.

"Do I have concerns? Absolutely I absolutely have concerns," Obama says. "He and I have many policy differences."

Several times Obama talked about the importance of how the new President staffs the White House, as Trump announces Steve Bannon, who is considered a white supremacist and racist, as his chief strategist.

At the press conference another asked about the Paris Climate Agreement.

"Climate Change?" Obama says, "If Trump does not follow through our kids will be choked off."

So what insights can we take from President Obama as we prepare for vigilance and, when necessary, dissent? At the press conference Obama encouraged us to consider the ideals and principles that ensure the United States is inclusionary and not exclusionary. If we can hold to this ideal all others will fall into place.

At the anti-Trump Rally at Columbus Circle the crowd was unified in their commitment to this ideal.

"When We Stand United Hate Can't Divide Us," the niece of the mother with the little girl had written on her sign.

Protesters shouted, "The people united will never be defeated!" Over and over. "The people united will never be defeated!"

And by their dissent, they rejected the temptation to normalize Trump's descent into the American psyche.

Dissent. Be peaceful. Yes. But not silent. Dissent.

This chapter was originally published under the same title on the Garn Press web site in November 2016

I'M A SCIENTIST. THIS IS WHAT I'LL FIGHT FOR

JONATHAN FOLEY

Jonathan Foley is a World-Leading Environmental Scientist andExecutive Director of the California Academy of Sciences

The War on Science is more than a skirmish over funding, censorship, and "alternative facts". It's a battle for the future, basic decency, and the people we love.

Make no mistake: There is a War on Science[6] in America.

The White House not only denies obvious, empirical facts on a regular basis, but they have invented the Orwellian concept of *"alternative* facts". In the past, we simply called them "lies", but now they are used in the world's most powerful office. And that should scare all of us.

What's worse is that the White House and many members of Congress aren't just *anti-fact*, they are against the *pursuit* of facts, and have tried to place draconian restrictions on what federal scientists can research, publish, and even discuss. And god knows what will happen to our nation's long-standing investments in research and science education.

This attack on science, and on knowledge itself, goes beyond anything we have seen in America before. And it is not only dangerous to science, it is dangerous to our nation and the world.

But the War on Science has inspired a mighty backlash. Scientists are standing up against politicians. We've seen rogue Twitter accounts, hundreds of op-eds, and scientists announcing they are running for office. There will even be a March for Science[7] on April 22. It's a popular uprising, complete with heroes in white lab coats and park ranger uniforms.

But when I see these signs of protest, I feel worried. Is this the right approach? Are we truly connecting with the American people?

Sure, people are taking a stand *against* "alternative facts", cuts to research, and muzzling scientists. But what are we *for*?

To truly connect with people, I think scientists and their supporters need to paint a *positive* vision of the future, where science re-affirms its moral authority, articulates how it will help us, and advances a noble cause.

In other words: What is the *higher purpose* of American science? *And what will scientists work for, live for, and fight for?*

I can't answer for other scientists, but here's what I will fight for.

Keeping America Great, As It's Always Been

Until recently, science has enjoyed deep, bipartisan support from elected officials. Thoughtful leaders on both sides of the aisle–from Teddy Roosevelt to Truman, Kennedy to Nixon, George H.W. Bush to Obama–have used science to guide our country forward.

And those leaders knew what I know: America is at its best when science is accepted and helps us do great things. Science helped us defeat fascism, win the Cold War, end polio, feed the world, land on the moon, and crack the code of life. What could it do next?

The greatness of America is strengthened by science – it helps us lift people up, improve the human condition, and build a better world.

Our future is dependent on science. Will we embrace science again, solve the challenges of our time, and thrive? Or will we turn our backs on science and fail being a great nation, dooming our future?

"The greatness of America is strengthened by science –it helps us lift people up, improve the human condition, and build a better world."

The Future Of Our Planet

Science shows us the magnificence of our world. Our oceans hold beautiful coral reefs, bursting with life, gleaming through azure waters. Tropical rainforests teem with creatures, sights, and sounds. Here in California, we have giant redwoods, reaching skyward, drenched in mist. And off our shores, there are colossal whales, drifting in rich waters, raising their young and singing their ethereal songs.

Through the lens of science, these wonders stir the mind,

inspiring awe and wonder. They awaken our hearts and souls. We instinctively want to share them with the people we love. And preserving them is the greatest gift we can give our children.

But science also tells us that these wonders are at risk from widespread habitat loss, pollution, and climate change. Science shows us the planet is in trouble, even if many politicians ignore the evidence.

But all is not lost. Science shows us ways of building a sustainable future – by reinventing our energy system, agriculture, and cities. Science can build a future where people and nature thrive together, for generations to come. Ignoring science will doom us to an impoverished, degraded world. Our children deserve better than that, and only science points the way forward.

"Through the lens of science, these wonders stir the mind, inspiring awe and wonder. They awaken our hearts and souls."

The Human Family

Science also tells us that we are *all* part of the same species, a single human family. While some try to divide us along national, gender, racial, and ethnic lines, science shows us that this is folly.

Science teaches us that national boundaries mean nothing. They are arbitrary lines etched into maps by people in power. But the Earth doesn't care. The air, the oceans, and the species we share this planet with need no passports. Only humans worry about that. Frank Borman, an Apollo astronaut, said it well: *"When you're… looking back on earth… you're going to get a concept that maybe this really is one world and why the hell can't we learn to live together like decent people."*

Science also tells us that our old ideas about gender, sexuality, and race are wrong. We should love who we want, the way we want. This is normal. What's not is homophobia and racism. Science teaches us that these are small-minded prejudices, not worthy of our species.

> *"We should love who we want, the way we want."*

The People I Love

If we live long enough, many of the people we love will fall ill, and some will die. Science may not always offer a cure, but it offers a chance. Or a way to manage pain. Or the hope that, someday, others won't have to face such a fate.

This is personal for me. It probably is for you.

When I was a teenager, my mother died of amyotrophic lateral sclerosis (ALS), a truly terrible disease. Science didn't give her a cure, or even a treatment, but I am hopeful that, someday, science will help another family.

And we all know people who are battling cancer. For me, a dearest friend, a valued co-worker, and a young niece are facing the disease and an uncertain future. But science is giving them the tools to fight–including the latest in laser surgery, radiation, and chemotherapy. Science is giving the people I love a fighting chance, and I will always be grateful to the scientists who gave them this gift.

Let's be clear: those who conduct a War on Science are also declaring war on the people we love. If they get their way, people will die. And I'm going to fight to make sure that doesn't happen.

You should too.

"Let's be clear: those who conduct a War on Science are also declaring war on the people we love. If they get their way, people will die."

It's easy to think that the War on Science is a secondary concern in our unfolding political crisis. After all, the very fabric of American democracy is unraveling, and it might seem we don't have time to worry about science.

But the War on Science affects all of us, and the things we hold most dear–including the greatness of America, the future of our planet, the decency of our society, and the people we love. Without unbiased facts, an informed citizenry, and the free and open pursuit of truth, we cannot be the America we want to be.

"...the War on Science affects all of us, and the things we hold most dear–including the greatness of America, the future of our planet, the decency of our society, and the people we love..."

The pursuit of science offers us hope–hope that we will be a great nation, living on a thriving world, as decent, kind people, with the people we love.

That is a cause I'm willing to work for, live for, fight for, and yes, even die for. And I know I'm not alone.

This chapter was originally published under the same title on the Macroscope web site in February 2017

ON DONALD TRUMP, NELSON MANDELA, RACISM AND MAKING FRIENDS WITH YOUR ENEMIES

CHARLENE SMITH

Charlene Smith is a Journalist, Documentary Film Maker, Author and Biographer of President Nelson Mandela

I'm the sort of immigrant Donald Trump finds acceptable, blonde, attractive, accomplished, and with a British accent.

On the last point, come to think of it, most Americans would let me in.

This is where it gets difficult; I am South African-born. I've lived under neo-Nazis. Some apartheid presidents were jailed during the Second World War for active Nazi support[8], and the biggest spy ring ever uncovered in the U.S. was led by a South African Nazi[9]. My parents were racist, and my father, a bully. I was a kind child and when about eight-years-old, my siblings and

I were playing in a park. I saw three black children holding the diamond links of the fence, watching us.

"Come and play with us," I said.

"Our mother said we can't," the boy closest in age to me said.

"Oh come, it will be fine," I urged, and they, tempted by the colorful merry-go-round, the swings and slides, ran into the park. There we played until we heard sirens and saw police vehicles skid to a stop outside the park. Something terrible must have happened. We stood transfixed. The police ran toward us. We were confused, we hadn't seen any baddies.

They grabbed the three black children, who screamed and cried, as they were hauled off to police vans. A black woman, a maid, came out of one of the houses and fell to her knees pleading with the police officers who ignored her.

She wailed as the police vehicles sped off.

I had done this. I brought harm to this mother and my friends. Even now I feel shame.

Children are wise, they understand injustice, and no matter what their parents say or do, they know.

I was a clever child who won academic and good fellowship awards at school, I was never promiscuous, nor used drugs or alcohol, but arguments at home intensified. I felt apartheid was unjust. At the age of sixteen, a month after I graduated high school, I was labelled a 'traitor' by my parents, and a 'kaffir boetie' (the equivalent of 'nigger lover') and banished from home. I had no money and scant education but a journalism cadet program at the largest newspaper group accepted this shy child. I became the youngest cadet reporter ever and the first woman crime reporter

in South African journalism. It was 1976 and black students protested inferior education. I saw the first dead bodies of my life as
children my age and younger were gunned down by police. More
than 600 died and that radicalized me. Five years later I was active
in the underground of the African National Congress, the outlawed
liberation group that Mandela belonged to.

There were three levels of commitment – were you prepared
to be arrested?

To prepare we read St. Augustine's *Just War* theory. I became
a disciple of Gandhi and satyagraha, non-violent resistance. He
counselled that we should not respond to haters in like manner
– or as Michelle Obama put it, "when they go low, we go high."
Gandhi also wrote in his 1928 book, *Satyagraha in South Africa*,
"you shall not bend your knee before an oppressor." Stand tall, be
dignified, never cower.

The next decision was, if I get arrested and am interrogated
and tortured, will I speak, or remain silent, or give them a little
but not that which is most important? Do I shame the oppressor
by carrying the harm in my own body, as Gandhi suggested? The
apartheid government loved torture as much as Trump.

The last personal assessment was, am I prepared to die?
Nelson Mandela said in his statement from the dock:

> We, of the ANC, always stood for a non-racial democ-
> racy. We shrank from any action which might drive the
> races further apart … Fifty years of non-violence brought
> the African people nothing but more and more repressive
> legislation, and fewer and fewer rights … Our complaint
> is not that we are poor by comparison with people in
> other countries, but that we are poor by comparison with
> white people in our own country. … I have cherished

the ideal of a democratic and free society in which all persons will live together in harmony and with equal opportunities. It is an ideal for which I hope to live for and to see realized. But, My Lord, if it needs be, it is an ideal for which I am prepared to die.

He was influenced by "Letter to a German Friend, July 1943," in *Resistance, Rebellion and Death,* by Albert Camus, which was published by Alfred A. Knopf in 1963. (I have the copy Mandela used.) These were letters the French Resistance dropped over German lines. Camus ends with words we need to start with:

This country is worthy of the difficult and demanding love that is mine. And I believe she is decidedly worth fighting for since she is worthy of a higher love... Your nation ... received... only the love it deserved, which was blind. A nation is not justified by such love. That will be your undoing. And you who were already conquered in your greatest victories, what will you be in the approaching defeat?

The U.S.A. is not worthy of blind love. I love it with my eyes open. I hear the fear of the white working class who have lost work, forfeited homes, status, and struggle to pay excessive interest rates on student loans. Hate is a product of fear. Always.

I am disturbed by the militarization of the police. The notion of service is being surrendered to police force, and this enables the shooting of too many black men.

I didn't want my children to live in a society that discriminated against anyone for any reason. I didn't want them to ask when they grew up, "what did you do mommy?" And to have no answer.

My road led to Nelson Mandela.

We left South Africa for a time because my American husband feared that he would be deported and I would be jailed. In 1989, I returned after the assassination of a close friend.[10] Four months later, Archbishop Desmond Tutu[11] asked if I would begin the first investigations into government death squads. God blessed us, because within two weeks a death squad assassin[12] escaped the noose in Pretoria by giving us an affidavit of some of his crimes. Liberal lawyers brought a stay of execution. It was my task to prove or disprove his claims before making them public. We did not know if this was security police disinformation. It included claims of police officials torturing a man then putting him on a spit to burn to death, while they barbecued nearby. They locked the doors of minivans with students inside and firebombed them. They used waterboarding, the helicopter, electric shock torture – all devices that the U.S.A. employs and we've mostly turned our faces because it was to others. It never could happen to us. Could it?

Pastor Niemoller[13], interned at Auschwitz wrote:

"First they came for the Socialists, and I did not speak out –

Because I was not a Socialist.

Then they came for the Trade Unionists, and I did not speak out –

Because I was not a Trade Unionist.

Then they came for the Jews, and I did not speak out –

Because I was not a Jew.

Then they came for me – and there was no one left to speak for me."

On February 10, 1990, I visited a friend recovering from pneumonia, Cyril Ramaphosa, now deputy president of South Africa. He was reading Barbara Tuchman's, *The March of Folly,* and said, "every politician must read this." In it, Barbara Tuchman writes:

> Folly is a child of power... The overall responsibility of power is to ...keep mind and judgement open and to resist the insidious spell of wooden-headedness. If the mind is open enough to perceive that a given policy is harming rather than serving self-interest, and self-confident enough to acknowledge it, and wise enough to reverse it, that is a summit in the art of government.

On February 11, 1990, Nelson Mandela, aged 71, walked free. Cyril held the microphone for him at his first public address in Cape Town. Two days later I was the second journalist to interview him in Soweto. He had such grace. Before I began he said, "Ms. Smith, I have read your works, I want to know about you." He quoted verbatim things I'd written years before, and asked me to describe persons or events.

Nelson Mandela was always interested. He cared. If he met you once, he would remind you, when next you met, of what you discussed six months or a year before.

The world loved Nelson Mandela because he loved us, all of us. He came out of prison and told South Africa's deeply divided people to 'make friends of your enemies' – when at that time there were government death squads, the right-wing were planting bombs at taxi ranks, and internecine violence saw hundreds of people die a week.

His approach caused anger among some ANC leaders. He listened to them patiently, and then asked, "What will it cost to negotiate?" They had no answer. We had lost so much peace was the most radical action of all.

No one was invisible to him. Our Madiba would arrive at an event and first greet the cooks, the cleaners, the security detail, the waiters; the rich and famous could wait. Everyone was important to him. Everyone is important.

He went to the white-only homeland of Orania to visit Betsy Verwoerd[14], the widow of the architect of apartheid and the man that sought Mandela's execution. When they emerged, his hand gently on her old shoulder, she looked at him with pleasure. It flabbergasted a nation of haters.

If a woman or child was gravely harmed, he would travel across the country to comfort them. He was our president, our best friend and trusted ally, regardless of our political persuasion. We called him Tata (father).

He wasn't perfect, he made mistakes, but he would admit when he was wrong, and change course. He was as flawed as we, he simply tried harder to be better.

I knew Nelson Mandela for 23 years. In July 2013, my father died and I did not mourn.

In 2015 I wrote a 'letter' ending with these words:

"I kept thinking about my absence of feeling. A few months after your death, Mandela died and I mourned deeply. I still do. At Christmas 2013, I thought of how sad your life was, how narrow, and how blessed I am to love many, and be loved by many. Sorrow for your sad life is what I now have, and so dad, my father, the architect of the person I am today, I want to thank you. I ope you have at last found peace."

In America today, we fear. People are angry. Friendships have splintered. People whisper behind closed doors. They have panic attacks or insomnia. As apartheid became more vicious I developed a stress-related heart condition that saw me in the I.C.U. a few times a year. Since moving to the U.S.A. I have never been hospitalized. Don't give bullies power over your mind and body.

I believe Mandela might say, "You know American people are very clever, they have achieved much. Along the way, they became lost, they were so busy telling others what to do that they ignored the cries of those at home. We are not ungrateful for their meddling, because sanctions – first called for by Martin Luther King in 1961 and finally defying a presidential veto from President Ronald Reagan in 1986 – saw me walk free less than four years later. As my good friend, the Archbishop Tutu might say, 'There is a time for everything, this is America's time, to build, to heal, to mend, to speak, to heal.'"

The word courage comes from the French word, coeur, it means heart. Courage comes from the heart. It is an act of love.

Open eyes are the fuel Lady Liberty needs. Pain leads to new awakenings, a fresh appreciation of what we are and all we can be. Listen with an open mind. Courage demands we make friends of our enemies and denounce persecutors. And always, as Mandela did, make time to dance.

Freedom challenges us. Justice Jackson ruled in 1941 in *West Virginia State Board of Education v. Barnette* (who refused to salute the flag), "Freedom to differ is not limited to things that do not matter much. That would be a mere shadow of freedom. The test of its substance is the right to differ as to things that touch the heart of the existing order."

After receiving a Congressional Gold Medal on October 6, 1994 – 14 years before being removed from the Terrorism Watch List[15] – President Nelson Mandela said: "At the end, goodwill prevailed. At the end, the overwhelming majority, both black and white, decided to invest in peace." This is my prayer for the land that has given hope to so many. In years to come may you look back at the courage you found, and the enhanced love you have for our *United* States of America.

"SALEM AND TRUMP: THE POWER OF FEAR IN 1692 AND 2016"

DAVID JOSEPH KOLB

David Joseph Kolb is a Prize Winning Reporter, Editor and Columnist, and Author of "Devil Knows: A Tale of Murder and Madness in America's First Century" (Garn Press)

The political use of fear, against which President Franklin Delano Roosevelt properly warned Americans in the face of the Great Depression and the looming menace of world fascism, is nothing new.

In fact, it's a common blood-red thread running throughout American history, from our "first century" – the 1600s – to this latest year.

Weaponized fear tactics have been used to hang women in the 1600s, accelerate the slaughter and disenfranchisement of Native Americans in the 1700s, provoke a Civil War in the 1800s, demonize liberalism in the 1900s and, finally and perhaps with the most dire consequences of all to follow, drive facts-confused presidential voters into the arms of a demagogue in 2016.

The first and most memorable of these assaults on the anxieties of an innocent population was the notorious Salem "witchcraft" hysteria of 1692. This fraud was in fact instigated by a deliberate fear campaign that stampeded the fertile imaginations of New Englanders into a frenzy of false accusations and, ultimately, murder.

Roosevelt, an accomplished politician himself, saw first-hand the Nazi and Stalinist mastery of propaganda used to bend the public will to its bidding.

The president understood that inciting fear and wielding it as a political weapon is designed to overwhelm common sense and stampede public opinion.

To his eternal credit, Roosevelt called "freedom from fear" one of the four basic human rights worth fighting for.

***

Provoking fear in the unreasoning mind is a powerful drug but one that wears off when the spell is broken. Lamentably, however, the damage done in its name remains a dark blot on the collective memories of the survivors.

How else to account for the ongoing popularity in the public imagination of the witch mania of 1692 in Salem, Massachusetts and throughout New England? For more than three centuries the outrages committed in Salem have exerted an unholy fascination on American culture out of all proportion to its fatal impact on the victims of that particular crime.

Certainly, the lives of those 20 innocents – for none was guilty of what they were accused – mattered. But is it only that gross miscarriage of justice that holds our interest all these years later?

You could put 1,000 Native American lives, snuffed out by murderers who were never held to account before the bar of justice, next to each of those strangled New Englanders and still not be square with the true count of loss, not even close.

And if one could unbury 10 times that number of black men, women and children, worked to death in slave days, or crushed out of all memory by the grinding brutality of racism in this seemingly endless post-Civil War era, there would be all too many dead still missing from the equation, not to mention human memory.

So if it is not about the numbers, what is it about the witch hunts that so supremely still commands our attention, almost to the exclusion of the other fear-driven campaigns of the past?

The answer lies in the terrifying ease with which fear manipulated a gullible public to acquiesce to crimes against law and reason that it would never countenance otherwise.

In Salem-era New England, the power of fear was magnified to such an extent that it drove a community of like-minded co-religionists into a condition of temporary insanity.

Puritans in that summer of 1692 under the thrall of the descriptive powers of the supreme witch-hunter of his time, the Rev. Cotton Mather, were absolutely convinced that a plot to destroy them was afoot in their colony and that Devil's hand – literally, Devil himself – was conniving to murder them and enslave their souls.

In order to accomplish this, went the story Mather and his fellow pastors spread, Devil needed willing accomplices within the communities he sought to destroy. The question that puzzled and worried so many that summer was who among their number would aid such a blasted conspiracy?

The introduction of unreliable evidence accepted as fact, the willingness of learned and respected peers to participate in the mad hunt, the absence of credible media, and the limited education of a public unwilling to question authority, all combined to provide the fuel necessary for the witch-hunt.

Once the flame caught, the mania to uncover these unholy covens was an idea that spread throughout the northern colonies like a plague, resulting in victims caught up in the net of suspicion and then convicted based upon evidence so flimsy that, when examined by the lights of a more reasoning moment in time, would appear ludicrous were the end results not so tragic.

***

Today, with Salem now centuries removed, a nervous world quells at the ascension of one Donald J. Trump to the presidency of the United States.

It is only fair to state that fear among many of his own fellow citizens was their most prevalent driving emotion to "vote Trump."

The idea that a greedy, paranoid, immoral serial liar and sexual predator would be taking charge of the machinery of government of the most powerful nation on earth, a concept both preposterous and awe-inspiring to many, was ignored by Trump voters who saw him only as their Great Protector from their many fears.

It's a disconnect not so odd when viewed in the light of history that tells us when the power of fear-mongering waxes full, common sense and reason wane – and make no doubt about it, the power of fear helped elevate Trump to this singular place of honor.

Long before Citizen Trump became President-Elect Trump, the path had been well-prepared for the future resident of the White House. For decades, a virtual army of well-funded, right-wing propagandists has been selling the lie that the Democratic Party and especially its liberal and progressive core are the enemies of America. Since there has been little concerted pushback or counter to this onslaught, almost half the nation's voters take the "Democrats are the enemy" lie as gospel.

An entire news network, Fox, has been devoted to pushing Trump-like principles and ideas – long before Trump was even a gleam in voters' eyes. And one can travel the length and breadth of the United States and never be more than a twitch of the radio dial away from the angry voices of far-right screamers warning of this or that Democratic, liberal plot, whatever that might be at any given moment.

Ironically, these purveyors of fear, pitting American against American, are themselves funded largely by the power of fear. Commercials promising relief from crime, bankruptcy and impotency help pay the freight for these programs. Meanwhile, the Democratic investment in public education is under attack, as is the teaching profession itself, since those who help open young minds to critical thinking, and prod them to ask questions and consult the history books of their local libraries are also viewed as suspects in the grand conspiracy.

The newspaper-reading public, what remains of it now, has been almost as ill served.

Corporate acquisition of independent papers has led to the dominance of newspaper chains and the rise of a media oligarchy that has put many daily publications into the same boat – a leaking one.

Poor decisions and ignorance about the Internet during the 1990s weakened newspaper revenues, leading to cutbacks in content, declining readership and ultimately the kicking of tens of thousands of trained journalists to the curb in search of new employment.

The once-numerous editorial pages of American newspapers, representing the snarling of those precious Fourth Estate watchdogs so beloved by the Founding Fathers, have largely been silenced for fear of angering the dwindling advertising base.

Book-reading, too, is taking the hit. Bookstores are endangered, as are small publishers. Americans increasingly get their ideas and even news from social media, a medium ripe for assault by "fake news" outlets, and hence about as informative as the gossip of old Salem.

Trump was able to exploit this national decline in the power of reason through his own use of the power of fear, revving up suppressed hatred and native prejudices, long in existence, against Muslims, Mexicans, African-Americans, feminists and intellectuals.

His promises of new greatness and wealth for the nation, backed up by nothing but empty rhetoric, went down easily among supporters predisposed to believe whatever they were told, and ineffective opposition arguments only cemented such support.

***

When fear is dominant, injustice reigns.

We know this because history cries to us that this is the result when reason fails, when ignorance prevails over education and, most disturbingly, when the old truths are ridiculed and laid aside.

Why does the power of fear triumph when the lessons of history warn us to beware?

It is because it is essential human nature to cling to the idea that protection from the demons without is possible only within the thrall of the loudest voices among us.

Screaming, shouting, strutting dictators who promise everything have long been the stuff of derision and scorn among Americans who once had everything, and who, comparatively, wanted for nothing.

The attack on America of 9/11 in 2001, coming so soon after one of the most controversial elections and Supreme Court rulings in history seemed to change all that. Suddenly, a "mandate" could be declared when there was none, drawn up in order "to protect us."

Fear won. The Bush Administration of that era changed not only our politics, but the way in which America saw itself, no longer independent, uncowed, optimistic – but frightened, fearful and anxious. Under that administration, the national economy almost crashed due to mismanagement and greed, bringing misery to millions and wounds that have remained unhealed.

That rescue was possible was because enlightenment resurfaced briefly – as it sometimes does – in our body politic, like Camelot of Arthur's day.

But Arthur could not prevail forever.

And after Nov. 8, 2016, the long eclipse of reason has resumed.

The end result can only be, as history has warned us when citizens desire answers and reassurance from those who mean them harm, that the old, familiar demons of our past will once more be set free to ravage the land.

It remains the duty of the rest of us to carry the lamplight of reason and truth forward into the new darkness at whatever cost, and to protect it for those who come after.

For once that light is extinguished, is there any guarantee it will ever be relit?

ZOMBIE POLITICS AND ALL THE BIG LIES REBORN IN TRUMPLANDIA

P.L. THOMAS

P.L. Thomas is a Recipient of the NCTE George Orwell Award and Author of "Beware the Roadbuilders" and "Trumplandia" (Garn Press)

The original zombie narrative[16] has been re-created and distorted in contemporary U.S. pop culture, as Victoria Anderson explains:[17]

So what were zombies, originally? The answer lies in the Caribbean. They weren't endlessly-reproducing, flesh-eating ghouls. Instead, the zombie was the somewhat tragic figure of a human being maintained in a catatonic state – a soulless body – and forced to labour for whoever cast the spell over him or her. In other words, the zombie is – or was – a slave. I always find it troubling that, somewhere along the line, we forgot or refused to acknowledge this and have replaced the suffering slave

with the figure of a mindless carnivore – one that repro-
duces, virus-like, with a bite.

While there is some nuance and variety among the many ways
in which U.S. pop culture have manipulated the zombie narrative,
central to almost all of those is the zombie as relentless consumer
who has risen from the dead and resists being killed permanently.

In that context and with the rise of Trumplandia, school
choice is zombie politics because the ideology will not die and its
many versions (vouchers, tuition tax credits, charter schools) are
destructive. A few decades ago, school choice advocacy depended
on the appeal of the ideology itself since choice is idealized and
fetishized in the U.S.

Once school choice policy began to be implemented, and
then over the past 2-3 decades as evidence from how choice has
not achieved the promises made, school choice advocacy has
depended on constantly shifting the *type* of choice and the *promises*.[18] At the center of the school choice debate is a failure in the
U.S. to appreciate the importance of the Commons, how publicly
funded institutions are necessary for the free market to work (both
economically and ethically).

For example, publicly funded roads and highways are powerful and essential for commerce in the U.S. Many resist toll roads
in the U.S., and certainly, the entire economy and way of life in
the U.S. would be destroyed if we left roads and highways to the
whims of the Invisible Hand. Two facts remain important now as
the election of Donald Trump and his nomination for Secretary
of Education suggest that the zombie politics of school choice has
been rejuvenated:

- The overwhelming evidence for all aspects of school choice
  show little differences when compared to traditional public

schools; some aspects can certainly be categorized as harmful, and any so-called positives are erased when those gains are explained – attrition, comparing apples and oranges, selectivity, inability to scale, etc.

- Idealizing parental choice fails to step back to the bedrock promise of publicly funded institutions: insuring that choice isn't necessary.

Just as a blow to the head and brain can kill permanently the zombie, evidence and truth should eradicate the zombie politics of school choice. However, Trumplandia is a post-truth[19] country.

How the media and politics have failed universal public education and education reform now represents the current state of the future of education and reform as well as the larger post-truth reality of U.S. politics and public discourse – all of which feeds zombie politics. In other words, the U.S. must confront that the rise of Trumplandia is not new, but a logical result of who we have always been in the U.S.

Mainstream Media, Not Fake News, Spawned Trumplandia

Some in the public thinking business have posited that Donald Trump is not a half-cocked loon, but a brilliant manipulator of the media, and thus the entire U.S., over which he now presides. Their basis for these claims is showing how he has artfully shot out Tweets perfectly timed to overshadow, these pundits argue, more substantive issues that the media should be addressing. Although I am not sure if I buy these pronouncements about Trump, I am certain about the power of *distraction*, especially as that contributes to zombie politics.

While the same punditry setting out to deconstruct Trumplandia claims that fake news is itself the distraction, as Sarah Ken-dzior confronts,[20] the histrionics about fake news are distracting us from a very real and very ugly truth[21]: having crossed the Bigfoot line,[22] mainstream media, not fake news, spawned Trumplandia.

Let me illustrate.

Consider the lede from Woman A Leading Authority On What Shouldn't Be In Poor People's Grocery Carts:[23]

> With her remarkable ability to determine exactly how others should be allocating their limited resources for food, local woman Carol Gaither is considered to be one of the foremost authorities on what poor people should and should not have in their grocery carts, sources said Thursday.

From 2014, this is satire from *The Onion*, a publication in the broad family of fake news (although satire has not the malicious intent of the more recently purposefully placed fake news designed to be click-bait and make money[24]).

What this satirizes, however, is incredibly important since it challenges the mostly misguided and nasty stereotypes[25] that many if not most Americans *believe* about people who are poor: it is the fault of the poor, laziness, that they are impoverished, and thus, they do not deserve the same things hard working people do deserve (as in luxuries such as sweets). We might argue that no reasonable person would believe a story from *The Onion* to be true, but it happens,[26] and well before all the hand-wringing about fake news and presidential politics.

Yet, what is far more disturbing is that despite concurrent charges the sky is falling because the expert is dead,[27] the U.S. still functions with an expert class of media, the primary cable news networks such as Fox and CNN as well as the last surviving newspapers, notably *The New York Times*. Yes, many may cast aspersions on the "liberal media," but concurrently, many people remain solidly faithful that the NYT is reporting credibly. And here is the irony: the NYT and mainstream media are overwhelmingly meeting the standards of mainstream media, and those standards of "both sides" and objective journalism are far more harmful and dangerous than fake news.

Just one week before Trump's inauguration, the NYT published In the Shopping Cart of a Food Stamp Household: Lots of Soda,[28] which in only a few days prompted this from state government:[29]

> A lawmaker in Tennessee wants to ban people from using food stamps to buy items that have no nutritional value. The bill[30] was proposed by Republican Rep. Sheila Butt.[31] *…

> House Bill 43 would prohibit people from using food stamps to purchase items high in calories, sugar or fat, according to the Tennessean.[32] That would include soda, ice cream, candy, cookies and cake.

However, there is more *indirect* truth in the satirical *The Onion* article than in the NYT article, as Joe Soss reports:[33]

> In a New York Times story[34] over the weekend, Anahad O'Connor massages and misreports a USDA study to reinforce some of the worst stereotypes about food stamps. For his trouble, the editors placed it on the front page. Readers of the newspaper of record learn that the end result of tax dollars spent on food assistance is a grocery cart full of soda. No exaggeration. The inside headline for the story is "What's in the Shopping Cart of a Food Stamp Household? Lots of Sugary Soda," and the

front-page illustration shows a shopping cart containing almost nothing but two-liter pop bottles.

Note the key words above are "misreports" and "stereotypes." Soss explains:

> Let's be clear here: this is nonsense. It's a political hack job against a program that helps millions of Americans feed themselves, and we should all be outraged that the New York Times has disguised it as a piece of factual news reporting on its front page.

> There are two major problems here. First, O'Connor misrepresents the findings of the USDA report. Second, O'Connor's article is a case study in the dark arts of making biased reporting appear even-handed. Let's start with the facts.

Not as sexy, and not what the general public believes, the USDA report actually has a much different message:

> A November 2016 study[35] by the U.S. Department of Agriculture examined the food shopping patterns of American households who currently receive nutrition assistance through the Supplemental Nutrition Assistance Program (SNAP) compared with those not receiving aid. Its central finding? "There were no major differences in the expenditure patterns of SNAP and non-SNAP households, no matter how the data were categorized."

Vallas and Robins note as well that the NYT/O'Connor misreporting is about more than feeding misguided stereotypes about people in poverty:

> Beyond the article's inaccuracies, there is a broader prob-

lem with this kind of reporting. It reinforces an "us versus them" narrative – as though "the poor" are a stagnant class of Americans permanently dependent on aid programs. The New York Times' own past reporting has shown that this simply isn't the case. Research by Mark Rank, which the paper featured[36] in 2013, shows that four in five Americans will face at least a year of significant economic insecurity during their working years. And analysis[37] by the White House Council on Economic Advisers finds that 70 percent of Americans will turn to a means-tested safety net program such as nutrition assistance at some point during their lives.

Now if we return to our current gnashing of teeth about the rise of fake news and the death of the expert, we should be confronting a couple far more pressing facts:

- Mainstream media are mostly conducting press-release journalism; are often bending to the market and not reaching for truth, justice, and the American way; and fail our democracy because of traditional norms of objectivity and "both sides" journalism.

- The public in the U.S. is not anti-expert, but seeking the *appearance* of expertise that confirms what they already believe – even when what they believe is total hogwash, and worse (racism, sexism, homophobia, etc.). **

Maybe we have a really ugly paradox here also: publications like *The Onion* and satirical programming such as work by John Oliver and *Saturday Night Live* are serving the American public and the ideal of democracy and freedom far better *as fake news* than even the so-called best mainstream media[38] are doing. Satirists are not bound to simplistic conventions of objectivity (ironically, to be neutral is to endorse the status quo), and are critical instead. Journalists refuse to embrace the power of a critical free press,[39] and thus, are eager to blame fake news, to use it as a distraction.

Finally, then, we must wonder with the recent revelations about plagiarism by Monica Crowley,[40] a popular rightwing expert, if O'Connor merely cribbed his NYT expose from *The Onion*, where three years ago they fabricated:

> "All that junk she's buying is just loaded with sugar, too," said Gaither, identifying with uncanny speed another critical flaw in her fellow shopper's grocery selection. "No wonder her kids are acting out like that."…

> "The other day, I saw a woman who bought a box of name-brand Frosted Flakes because, apparently, the generic kind wasn't fancy enough for her," said Gaither, swiftly and decisively calculating that bagged cereal would have cost half as much. "And guess who's going to be paying the difference in the end?"

A speculation that does make sense because reading *The Onion* is far more entertaining and informative than plowing through a government report.

The Big Lie about the Left in the U.S.

This blurring of the spectrum from fake news to mainstream journalism as well as how edujournalism has been a harbinger to the rise of Trumplandia will become manifest under Trump's perpetuating zombie politics with the Big Lie. As one example, the Big Lie about the Left in the U.S. is that the Left exists in some substantial and influential way in the country. The Truth about the Left in the U.S. is that the Left does not exist in some substantial and influential way in the country. Period.

The little lies that feed into the Big Lie include that universities and professors, K-12 public schools, the mainstream media,[41] and Hollywood[42] are all powerful instruments of liberal propaganda. These little lies have cousins in the annual shouting about the "war on Christmas" and hand wringing by Christians that they are somehow the oppressed peoples of the U.S. These lies little and Big are a scale problem in that the U.S. is now and has always been a country whose center is well to the right, grounded as we are in capitalism more so than democracy.

The U.S. is a rightwing country that pays lip service to progressivism and democracy; we have a vibrant and powerful Right and an anemic, fawning Middle. Wealth, corporatism, consumerism, and power are inseparable in the U.S. – pervading the entire culture including every aspect of government and popular culture. The Left in the U.S. is a fabricated boogeyman, designed and perpetuated by the Right to keep the general public distracted. Written as dark satire, Kurt Vonnegut's *Cat's Cradle*[43] now serves as a manual for understanding how power uses false enemies to maintain power and control.[44]

Notably during the past 30-plus decades, conservative politics have dominated the country, creating for Republicans a huge problem[45] in terms of bashing "big government."

But dog-whistle politics grounded in race and racism benefitting the Right and Republicans have a long history. In 1964,[46] Martin Luther King Jr. confronted[47] Barry Goldwater's tactics foreshadowing Trump's strategies and rise:

> **The Republican Party geared its appeal and program to racism, reaction, and extremism...** On the urgent issue of civil rights, Senator Goldwater represents a philosophy that is morally indefensible and socially suicidal. **While not himself a racist, Mr. Goldwater articulates a phi-**

losophy which gives aid and comfort to the racist. His candidacy and philosophy would **serve as an umbrella under which extremists of all stripes would stand.** In the light of these facts and because of my love for America, I have no alternative but to urge every Negro and white person of goodwill to vote against Mr. Goldwater and to withdraw support from any Republican candidate that does not publicly disassociate himself from Senator Goldwater and his philosophy.

Malcolm X held forth[48] in more pointed fashion, but with the same focus:

"Well if Goldwater ever becomes president one thing his presence in the White House will do, it will make black people in America have to face up [to] the facts probably for the first time in many many years," Malcolm X said.

"This in itself is good in that Goldwater is a man who's not capable of hiding his racist tendencies," he added. "And at the same time he's not even capable of pretending to Negroes that he's their friend."

The Civil Rights icon concluded that should Goldwater be elected, he would inspire black people to fully reckon with "whites who pose as liberals only for the purpose of getting the support of the Negro."

"So in one sense Goldwater's coming in will awaken the Negro and will probably awaken the entire world more so than the world has been awakened since Hitler," he said.

Mentioned earlier, the annual panic over the "war on Christmas" is a distraction from the fact that Christmas serves consumerism, the Right, and not religion – keeping in mind that Jesus and his ideology rejected materialism and espoused moral and ethical codes in line with socialism and communism/Marxism. What remains mostly unexamined is that all structures are essentially conservative – seeking to continue to exist. Power, then, is always resistant to change, what should be at the core of progressivism and leftwing ideology. Marxism is about power and revolution (drastic change, and thus a grand threat to power), but suffers in the U.S. from the cartoonish mischaracterization from the Right that it is totalitarianism.

So as we drift toward the crowning of the greatest buffoon ever to sit at the throne of the U.S. as a consumerocracy posing as a democracy, *Education Week* has decided to launch into[49] the hackneyed "academics are too liberal and higher education is unfair to conservatives" ploy, yet another form of zombie politics writ small. At the center of this much-ado-about-nothing is Rick Hess[50] playing his Bokonon and McCabe role:

> I know, I know. To university-based education research-ers, all this can seem innocuous, unobjectionable, and even inevitable. But this manner of thinking and talking reflects one shared worldview, to the exclusion of others. While education school scholars may almost uniformly regard a race-conscious focus on practice and policy as essential for addressing structural racism, a huge swath of the country sees instead a recipe for fostering grievance, animus, and division. What those in ed. schools see as laudable efforts to promote "equitable" school discipline or locker-room access strike millions of others as an ideological crusade to remake communities, excuse irre-sponsible behavior, and subject children to goofy social engineering. Many on the right experience university initiatives intended to promote "tolerance" and "diver-sity" as attempts to silence or delegitimize their views on immigration, criminal justice, morality, and social policy.

For readers who find it hard to believe that a substantial chunk of the country sees things thusly, well, that's kind of the issue.

Conversational and posing as a compassionate conservative, Hess sprinkles in scare quotes while completely misrepresenting everything about which he knows nothing. This is all cartoon and theater.

The grand failure of claiming that the academy is all leftwing loonies is that is based almost entirely – see the EdWeek analysis – on noting that academics overwhelmingly identify as Democrats. However, the Democratic Party is not in any way a substantial reflection of leftist ideology. At most, we can admit that Democrats tend to use progressive rhetoric (and this is a real characteristics of professors, scholars, and academics), but that Democratic policy remains centrist and right of center.

A powerful example of this fact is the Department of Education (DOE) and Secretary of Education (SOE) throughout George W. Bush's and Barack Obama's administrations.

For the past 16 years, education policy has been highly bureaucratic and grounded almost entirely in rightwing ideology – choice, competition, accountability, and high-stakes testing.

The only real difference between Bush's SOE and Obama's SOE has been rhetoric;[51] yes, Duncan, for example, loved to chime in with civil rights lingo, but policy under Obama moved *farther* right than under Bush. Now, let me address the charge that college professors are a bunch of leftwing loonies.

I can do so because I am the sort of dangerous professor[52] Hess wants everyone to believe runs our colleges and universities – poisoning the minds of young people across the U.S.

I can also add that I spent 18 years as a public school teacher before the past 15 years in higher education. In both so-called liberal institutions – public education and higher education – as a real card-carrying Lefty, I have been in the minority, at best tolerated, but mostly ignored and even marginalized. Public schools are extremely conservative, reflecting and perpetuating the communities they serve. In the South, my colleagues were almost all conservative in their world-views and religious practices.

My higher education experience has been somewhat different because the atmosphere has the veneer of progressivism (everyone know how to talk, what to say), but ultimately, we on the Left are powerless, unheard and often seen as a nuisance. Colleges and universities are institutions built on and dependent on privilege and elitism. As I noted above, colleges and universities are not immune to the conservative nature of institutions; they seek ways to maintain, to conserve, to survive. Thus, colleges and universities are also not immune to business pressures, seeing students and their families as consumers.

Do professors push back on these tendencies and pressures? Sure. But that dynamic remains mostly rhetorical. The Truth is that colleges and universities are centrist organizations – not unlike the Democratic Party and their candidates, such as Obama and Hillary Clinton.

Some progressives in the U.S. play both sides to sniff at the power on the Right, and then the Right uses that rhetoric and those veneers to prove how the Left has taken over our colleges/universities, public schools, media, and Hollywood.

But that is a Big Lie about the Left in the U.S.

The Left does not exist in any substantial way, except as a boogeyman controlled by the Right in order to serve the interests of those in power.

"To be afraid is to behave as if the truth were not true," Bayard Rustin warned.[53]

Vonnegut's *Cat's Cradle* dramatizes this warning, and 50 years ago King and Malcolm X challenged us to see beyond the corrosive power of dog-whistle politics.[54]

When the Right paints educational research as the product of corrupted leftwing scholars, you must look past the zombie politics and examine in whose interest it is that market-based education reform survives despite the evidence against it. To paraphrase Gertrude from *Hamlet*, "The Right protests too much, methinks," and we have much to fear from all these histrionics.

---

* I know this appears to read like a piece from *The Onion*, but Republican Rep. Sheila Butt is real; *The Onion* would have used Ophelia Butt.

** Consider that the century-old debate between Creationism and evolution has morphed into the rise of Intelligent Design (replacing creationism) as pseudo-science to battle with traditional science, evolution.

THE RED QUEEN

JENNIFER C. BERKSHIRE

Jennifer Berkshire is a Writer, Editor, and Author of the "Have You Heard" Blog and Co-Host of its Weekly Podcast on "Education in the Time of Trump"

The ultimate target of Betsy DeVos' agenda isn't teachers unions, or even the "education establishment." It's the Democratic Party...

By the measures that are supposed to matter, Betsy DeVos' experiment in disrupting public education in Michigan has been a colossal failure. In its 2016 report[55] on the state of the state's schools, Education Trust Midwest painted a picture of an education system in freefall. "Michigan is witnessing systematic decline across the K-12 spectrum...White, black, brown, higher-income, low-income – it doesn't matter who they are or where they live." But as I heard repeatedly during the week I recently spent crisscrossing the state, speaking with dozens of Michiganders, including state and local officials, the radical experiment that's playing out here has little to do with education, and even less to do with kids. The real goal of the DeVos family is to crush the state's teachers unions as a means of undermining the Democratic party, weakening Michigan's democratic structures along the way. And on this front, our likely next Secretary of Education has enjoyed measurable, even dazzling success.

This story goes back a long ways, so settle in. We could start in the 1840's, when the first Dutch settlers began to arrive in Western Michigan, or in 1970, when the DeVoses made their first attempt to amend the state constitution[56] so as to allow for public funding for private, religious schools. Another obvious starting point is 1993, when then Governor John Engler called the public schools in Michigan an "educational gulag" and a "monopoly of mediocrity," [57] lobbing the first fusillade in a war against the state's teachers that has never ceased. For the sake of brevity, though, I'll fast forward to the mid-oughts, when Betsy's husband Dick DeVos ran for governor. It was the fourth time that the DeVoses had brought their crusade to give the market and the Maker more sway over the state's schools to the voters, and each time Mitten staters had delivered a resounding "no thanks" in response. And so the DeVoses pivoted. If they couldn't convince voters to enact their favored policies, they'd purchase the legislature instead.

Michistan

A characteristic DeVos move in Lansing traces a familiar pattern. A piece of legislation suddenly appears courtesy of a family ally. It pops up late in the session, late at night, or better still, during lame duck, when the usual legislative horse trading shifts into overdrive. So it was with a controversial bill that popped up 2013, doubling the limits for campaign contributions[58] – a limit that no one in Michigan was wealthy enough to hit. Well almost no one. The GOP jammed the measure through, Governor Snyder signed it, and it took effect immediately. "The DeVoses then got their whole clan together and held a check writing party," recalls Jeff Irwin, a Democratic state representative from Ann Arbor who was recently term-limited out. "It was a love letter to the richest people in Michigan and they delivered with a huge thank you."

I was captivated by the image of the extended DeVos clan gathered on New Year's Eve 2013, writing check after check to Republican candidates and caucuses, to the tune of more than $300,000, an exercise they would repeat just a few months later. Did they sip champagne as they signed? Did their hands grow weary? For the DeVoses, the ability to give even more money means that they can exert even more influence. "When you empower a billionaire family like that, you give them more power," Michigan Campaign Finance Network director Craig Mauger told me when I stopped by to see him in Lansing. Just blocks from the Capital, his office is in a part of the city that teems with the lobbyists who hold so much sway here. His building is home to not one, but two different for-profit charter operators. "The DeVoses are tilting the field and changing the structures of politics in Michigan."

To understand why the DeVoses exert so much influence, and more importantly, why their power has only increased in recent years, a quick session in civics is required. Today's topic: term limits. Approved in 1992 by voters in a "throw out the bums" state of mind, term limits have radically reordered the state's political landscape. Legislators here can serve no more than three two-year terms in the House, and two four-year terms in the state Senate – the strictest limits in the country. "They're in office for such a short time that it doesn't pay off for them to build a strong base of support in their own districts," Steve Norton, the head of the public education advocacy group Michigan Parents for Schools, explained to me. Instead, legislators are highly dependent on the party machinery, down to being told which way to vote. "They salute and follow caucus orders," says Norton. As both the funders of the GOP machine, and its de facto operators, that means that the DeVoses essentially control the legislature these days. "They are the 800 lb gorilla."

Check mate

By now, you probably think that I'm exaggerating. That it is simply inconceivable that a state that in the 19th century led the way in creating a public K-16 system could come to be so dominated by a family that seems intent on blowing it up. But virtually no one I spoke with saw any chance of putting the brakes on the DeVoses and their agenda – at least until something is done about gerrymandering[59] and the state's notoriously inadequate campaign finance laws.[60] While Business Leaders for Michigan, a CEO group, has begun to cast a wary eye on what the DeVos-led experiment in choice unfettering is doing to the state's economic standing, they've avoided taking on the DeVoses and their allies, including the Chamber of Commerce, that have made the family's priorities their own. Meanwhile, the incoming legislature is even more conservative than the one it's replacing, as Gary Naeyaert from the Great Lakes Education Project (GLEP) pointed out to me with glee when we spoke late last year. GLEP, founded and funded by Betsy DeVos, backed 34 legislators in the last election, each of whom answered the "right" way on the group's candidate survey[61] – 30 of them won.

John Stewart, a former Republican state rep who now practices law in Plymouth, 25 miles west of Detroit, laughed out loud when I asked him if there is anyone in Michigan whom the DeVoses are afraid of. Stewart ran afoul of the DeVoses back in 2002 when he refused to cast a vote in favor of lifting the state's cap on charter schools. He got "taken to the woodshed," in Lansing parlance, and was told that Betsy DeVos had a $10,000 check for him if he voted the right way, and that unpleasantness lay ahead if he didn't.

He declined the money. "I'm not some prostitute for the sake of $10,000," says Stewart, who switched his party affiliation in 2007.

Like Betsy DeVos, Stewart hails from the western Michigan city of Holland. His mother was a VanDerVen, and seven of her twelve sisters were public school teachers, including one who was the very first special education teacher in the state. As Stewart told me when I visited him at his law office, former governor John Engler shared the DeVos' desire to destroy public education, but he was powerful enough to serve as an occasional counterweight to them. He was against their effort to amend the constitution to allow for vouchers because he saw it as a political loser. And when Betsy DeVos first sought to become chairwoman of the state Republican party in 2000, Engler resisted. "He thought she was too divisive and too extreme," says Stewart. Today, there isn't anyone left to say "no" to the DeVoses. The moderate wing of the GOP, still referred to here as Milliken Republicans[62] for the popular governor who ran the state from 1969 to 1983, barely exists. "They've been obliterated by the DeVoses," says Stewart.

Whatever happened to local control?

Several times during my tour of Michigan, I heard a story about some political development so over-the-top sounding, so preposterous seeming as to be unbelievable. Later on I'd look it up, only to discover that it was even worse than what had been described. Like Senate Bill 571, the so-called "gag order" law[63] intended to keep public entities from talking to their constituents about local ballot measures – school millages and bonds to fund public services. It came on the heels of another DeVos priority, a bill banning straight ticket voting in the state,[64] or rather in Detroit, where African American voters are overwhelmingly Democrats. Bill 571 arrived late one night at the end of the session in the form of a lengthy amendment put forward by a DeVos legislator.

Republicans were instructed by their caucus to vote for it but not allowed to read it. The judge who slapped an injunction on the measure did so because it was "unconstitutionally vague," not to mention absurd; officials who mentioned a ballot measure in a city newsletter within sixty days of an election could be prosecuted.

The law would have so hamstrung local school districts that Moody's issued a report deeming it "credit negative." And that was exactly the point, East Grand Rapids school board member Elizabeth Welch told me. "What better way to convince local communities that it's time to abandon their public schools, even the good ones, than to let their buildings fall apart?" Her district in the Republican stronghold of western Michigan, the DeVos' home base, was trying to pass a bond measure for its high school when Governor Snyder signed the new law. "You defund the schools, you undermine them, you expand choice for the sake of choice, all towards the ultimate goal of destroying public education," says Welch. As for local control, a supposed Republican tenet, you don't hear so much about it in Michigan these days. As one sitting legislator told me, the very words have all but disappeared from the Republican lexicon.

By the midpoint of my trip, I'd lost count of the number of people who had told me that the DeVoses were out to destroy public education in Michigan. More chilling though were the matter-of-fact recitations of just how much progress has been made towards realizing that goal. "Choice" in its myriad forms – charter schools, virtual schools, inter-district choice – has exploded across the state, leading to steep drops in student enrollment in two-thirds of school districts.[65] Districts that end up in the red now risk state takeover thanks to the long tentacles of the emergency management law.[66]

"They have succeeded in diminishing the public school establishment financially and weakening it," former State Board of Education member John Austin told me. He was referring to what a certain brand of education reformer refers to derisively as "the blob" – the teachers and their unions, the school boards and the superintendents – those who resist disruption because they have a stake in the schools, which in Michigan turns out to be just about everyone. Austin lost his Board seat in the last election, a casualty of the Trump wavelet. Ironically, the same straight-ticket voting that the Republicans recently tried to ban likely benefited them in November. Austin, who is mulling a run for governor, maintains that the DeVos' fierce push for a largely unregulated education marketplace is but a means to their ultimate goal. "This is about taking down the existing public school infrastructure and the Democratic party."

Back to the future

In 1968, Walter Reuther, the head of the mighty auto workers union, traveled from Detroit to Memphis to march with Martin Luther King Jr. and striking sanitation workers. On the eve of King's assassination, Reuther told the workers that the labor movement would drag Memphis into the 20th century. Tennessee, like most southern states, had enacted right-to-work legislation, what unions once called the "slave labor act." But as historian Jefferson Cowie points out in *The Great Exception: The New Deal and the Limits of American Politics*, Reuther's prediction was wrong. History moved the other way, and after the GOP wave election of 2012, right-to-work swept through the Midwest: Wisconsin, Indiana, and Michigan,[67] the state where the Flint sit-down strike of 1936 ushered in the era of industrial unionism.

There is no way to explain how "right to work" works without calling upon obscure union lingo – agency fee, closed shop, free riders, Taft-Hartley, Section 14(b) – not to mention the long, tortured history of US labor law. So I will bypass the "how" and proceed directly to the "why": right-to-work curtails the power of unions and keeps workers weak. It's a priority for those who would like to see an end to unions, which is why when the bill that enacted right-to-work in Michigan suddenly appeared late in 2012, bearing all of the hallmarks of a classic DeVos move (a lame duck session, no committee hearings, the gallery filled with GOP staffers so as to keep out the public), Betsy herself was reportedly on the chamber floor, corralling wavering legislators with the DeVos family recipe of largesse and threats.

In their excellent new book *A Fight for the Soul of Public Education* about the 2012 Chicago teachers strike, Bob Bruno and Steven Ashby explain that the call for the evisceration of what public sector workers can negotiate over isn't primarily about saving states money. "It is about blocking the ability of organized labor to translate workplace representation power into social and political power." This is where the DeVoses and their allies have been so successful. The terrain of what teachers in Michigan are allowed to bargain over has been drastically shrunk, with the aim of sending union members this message: "There is nothing your union can do you for you," in order that they should ask the logical follow-up question: "So why am I paying union dues?"

The union leaders I talked to were candid about how devastating the DeVos' efforts have been. The unbridled growth of charter schools, almost all of which are non-union, means that new teachers in the state are far less likely to be union members. In Detroit, for example, the once powerful Detroit Federation of Teachers is down to just 3,000 members from more than 9,000 a decade ago, while fully half of the teachers in the city are unorganized. Meanwhile, an array of new legislation has taken direct aim at the machinery of how unions are run. The same election law package enacted last year that included the "gag order" made it illegal for employers, including school districts, to process union dues, while simultaneously making it easier for corporations to deduct PAC money from employee paychecks.[68]

The DeVos' target is the unions' political war chest, and here too their handiwork has had its desired effect. With fewer resources to draw upon, the Michigan Education Association and the far smaller American Federation of Teachers, have less to give to candidates and political campaigns, to canvassing operations and phone banks, to get out the vote efforts and yard signs. During the most recent political cycle, the DeVos family outspent the two largest unions in the state, the UAW and the MEA, by a wide margin.[69] The tragedy of all of this if you are, as this author is, a believer in unions yet clear-eyed about their flaws, their forever falling-short-ness, and their infuriating hideboundedness, is that the loss of political influence in Michigan has made the unions more risk averse than ever. The state went big for Bernie in the primaries, its unions stuck with Hillary. On election night Trump won Michigan by a mere 10,000 votes.

A glimmer of hope

You need a reprieve at this point; I know, I did too. And so we will pause here to meet some teachers, and to remind ourselves that no matter how systematic and well-funded the assault on collective action and democracy may be,[70] the impulse to fight back, to resist, is almost impossible to quash completely. Asenath Jones, Vanessa Dawson, Stephanie Griffin and Lacetia Walker all teach in Detroit, and while you may not know them, you know *of* them. They helped to organize the sick-outs last year to call attention to, well, everything that's befallen the Detroit schools, their students and their teachers. Protests had been happening in a scattered form for months, but then former Flint emergency manager Darrell Earley, the same guy who oversaw that city's switchover to

Flint River water before being appointed emergency manager for the Detroit public schools, called out the teachers as unethical.[71]

"That was the last straw," says Dawson. She texted her colleagues, who texted their colleagues, and when organizers held a conference call, more than 1,000 teachers phoned in. The following week, teachers at some sixty schools refused to report to work. At its peak, the sick-outs shut down 94 of the city's 97 schools.[72] Media reports routinely characterized the protests as being about appalling school conditions – mushrooms! mold! – and the outrageous demand by the teachers that they be paid for their work. That was partly true, says Griffin, but the sick-outs were about so much more. The teachers were sounding a collective "enough" to endless cuts, closures and punishments, and to the entire thrust of education policies, dreamed up in Lansing and directed at Detroit. Says Griffin: "The assumption is that black and brown teachers aren't prepared to teach, and black and brown kids aren't prepared to learn."

Griffin started out teaching at charter schools here, then moved to Detroit's Education Achievement Authority when it was just getting off the ground, lured in part by a starting salary $20,000 higher than what new Detroit teachers make. But what she saw appalled her – "they were basically using minority kids to test software"[73] – and she worked with other teachers to shut the EAA down. Griffin was also part of the Coalition for the Future of Detroit's School Children, the group that pushed for Detroit to have more of a say over its schools, garnering the support of the city's mayor, the civic elites and the *Detroit Free Press*, before running smack into the DeVos buzz saw last summer.[74]

Now she is part of a group within the union that calls itself "Detroit Teachers for Fairness and Equity." Their mission, as fellow member Asenath Jones describes it, is "to lead our union back to greatness." They are what education reformers might call teacher leaders, and they are all too aware that their skills and knowledge would command far more pay if they gave up on on Detroit and decamped for the suburbs. But for now they're hanging in and fighting on.

If you ain't Dutch, you ain't much

It was time for me to head west, to Michigan's second capital: Grand Rapids. I took the DeVos Place exit, passing by the DeVos Place Convention Center and the DeVos Performance Hall. At the Amway Grand Plaza Hotel, I stood in rapt awe before the enormous portraits of Richard DeVos Sr. and his Amway cofounder, Jay Van Andel. I went to Ada, home to Dick and Betsy, and to the sprawling headquarters of Amway, the multi-level marketing behemoth that is now enriching its third generation of DeVoses. And at Grand Valley State University, I walked along the Edgar D. Prince promenade, named for Betsy's father, who made his fortune manufacturing dashboard cup holders and lighted visor mirrors, and whose rabid anti-New Deal vision his daughter is so successfully carrying out today.

I was headed to Grand Valley's charter schools office, part of the powerful nexus of DeVos money, charter schools and lobbyists that is increasingly determining the future of Detroit's schools, and by extension, the city itself. This was to be my very last interview, and I'd been tempted to cancel it. My meeting with the Michigan Association of Public School Academies earlier in my trip had been testy to the point of acrimony, and on this, the eighth day of my adventure, I knew that my good behavior reserves were running dangerously low. Tim Wood, who oversees Grand Valley's charter schools office, and Rob Kimball, the deputy director, would be my 42nd and 43rd interviews. But charter authorizers play a huge role in Michigan's choice landscape, and Grand Valley is the state's largest, having authorized 73 schools serving 33,000 students. Besides, I'd never met an actual authorizer before.

We talked for almost an hour and a half. They made the case that Michigan's regulatory woes have been overstated, and that it's time to leave behind the assumption that "for-profit" is bad; more than half of their schools are part of the for-profit National Heritage Academies network. While there were a few tense moments, like when Kimball, who oversees Grand Valley's Detroit "portfolio," alleged that they are stakeholders in the city because they maintain an office there, these were the exception. The conversation was far more candid than I'd expected; at one point Kimball stated that charter expansion has brought the Detroit Public Schools to its knees. We discussed Betsy DeVos only briefly. Wood said that he was excited about her appointment; that she's thought about children most of her career. "It's inaccurate to say that she wants to hurt public schools," he said. "She likes schools that serve kids well."

I sensed no particular conviction behind his words, though, and frankly I was tired of talking about Betsy DeVos, so I let it drop. After a while, we just chatted. I told them about where I'd been and who I'd talked to, and that I'd just received an alert from my father, an expert on all subjects, urging me to look into the great Grand Rapids furniture strike of 1911. I was gathering up my things to go when Kimball asked me why it is that Democrats in Michigan are opposed to charter expansion, unlike in so many other states where the cause is bipartisan.

I told him what I'd been hearing all week. That in Michigan it is far more obvious that the Democrats themselves are the ultimate target of the effort to undermine public education. I resisted the urge to editorialize on why I think DeVos represents such a threat to a bipartisan education reform agenda that has bound together Republicans who'd like to crush unions with Democrats who want to weaken them "for the right reasons." Or that characterizing DeVos as "anti-accountability" misses how eagerly she and her allies embraced Obama's education reforms when they realized they'd just been given new tools with which to go after public schools and their teachers.

"Kneecapping the unions isn't the ultimate goal," I said. "They want to take out the teachers unions because they provide the foot soldiers that get Democrats elected. This is about making Michigan a red state."

Kimball looked genuinely startled. Outside it had started to snow and I hoped it wasn't the beginning of the ice storm that was supposed to sweep across the Upper Midwest; I was flying home in the morning.

"Can't we just find new foot soldiers?" Kimball asked.

I didn't have an answer. I'm not sure anyone does.

This chapter was originally published under the same title on the author's "Have You Heard" blog (formerly the "EduShyster" blog) in January 2017

HOW BIG DATA BECOMES PSY OPS AND TILTS THE WORLD TOWARDS ITS OWN AIMS: NEXT STOP, PUBLIC EDUCATION

MORNA MCDERMOTT

Morna McDermott is Professor of Education and Co-Editor of "Testing Our Courage: United Opt Out and the Testing Resistance Movement"

The psy ops tactics used to get Donald Trump elected to the U.S. Presidency (still having gag reflex) are the same ones being used in public schools, using children as their "data" source. Given the power they had on influencing the electorate, imagine what they could do with 12 years of public school data collected on your child.

What data? And how was it used?

In a January, 2017 report "The Data That Turned the World

Upside Down" in *Motherboard*,[75] Hannes Grassegger and Mikael Krogerus describe how a psychologist named Michael Kosinski and his co-worker David Stillwell at Cambridge University beginning in 2008 developed an application they named "MyPersonality" to analyze Facebook members using different psychometric questionnaires. Dr. Kosinski is a leading expert in psychometrics, a data-driven sub-branch of psychology. His work is grounded on the "Five Factors of Personality" theory, which are often called OCEAN, an acronym for Openness, Conscientiousness, Extraversion, Agreeableness, and Neuroticism. By 2014 what had started as a fun experiment for Kosinski and Stillwell had become the largest data set combining psychometric scores with Facebook profiles ever collected.

So many people volunteered their personal information to play these games and take these quizzes that before long Kosinski had volumes of data from which he could now predict all sorts of things about the attitudes and behaviors of these individuals. He applied the "Five Factors" (Big Five Theory) model (well-known in psychometric circles) and developed a system by which he could predict very personal and detailed behaviors of individuals on a level deeper than had been possible by prior models or systems.

Enter a British firm called Strategic Communication Laboratories (SCL)[76], which provides governments, political groups and commercial companies around the world with services ranging from military disinformation campaigns to social media branding and voter targeting. According to the *Motherboard* report, Kosinski was approached in 2014 by another Cambridge University researcher Aleksandr Kogan:

> He said was inquiring on behalf of a company [SCL] that was interested in Kosinski's method, and wanted to access the MyPersonality database. Kosinski Googled

the company: "[We are] the premier election management agency," says the company's website. SCL provides
marketing based on psychological modeling. One of its
core focuses: Influencing elections. Influencing elections? Perturbed, Kosinski clicked through the pages.
What kind of company was this? And what were these
people planning?

Kosinski apparently did not know the worldwide reach and
election involvement of the SCL group of companies, nor at that
time did he know about Alexander James Ashburner Nix, the
CEO of another British company Cambridge Analytica,[77] a company spun off by SCL in 2013 "to participate in US elections." The
Motherboard report states that:

> Kosinski knew nothing about all this, but he had a bad
> feeling. "The whole thing started to stink," he recalls.
> On further investigation, he discovered that Aleksandr
> Kogan had secretly registered a company doing business
> with SCL. According to a December 2015 report in *The
> Guardian* and to internal company documents given to
> *Das Magazin*, it emerges that SCL learned about Kosin-
> ski's method from Kogan. Kosinski came to suspect that
> Kogan's company might have reproduced the Facebook
> "Likes"-based Big Five measurement tool in order to
> sell it to this election-influencing firm. He immediately
> broke off contact with Kogan and informed the director
> of the institute, sparking a complicated conflict within
> the university…. Then, in November 2015, the more radi-
> cal of the two Brexit campaigns, "Leave.EU," supported
> by Nigel Farage, announced that it had commissioned
> Cambridge Analytica to support its online campaign. …
> After the Brexit result, friends and acquaintances wrote
> to him: Just look at what you've done. Everywhere he

went, Kosinski had to explain that he had nothing to do with this company.

In a December, 2016 article[78] *The Guardian* described recent research by Jonathan Albright, an assistant professor of communications at Elon University in North Carolina. Albright started with a list of 306 right wing news sites that were circulating fake news, and then examined and mapped them to see where their links went – into YouTube and Facebook, and between each other. Albright was astounded at what he found:

> [There were] millions of them... and I just couldn't believe what I was seeing. They have created a web that is bleeding through on to our web. This isn't a conspiracy. There isn't one person who's created this. It's a vast system of hundreds of different sites that are using all the same tricks that all websites use. They're sending out thousands of links to other sites and together this has created a vast satellite system of rightwing news and propaganda that has completely surrounded the mainstream media system. ... it actually looks like a virus. And Facebook was just one of the hosts for the virus that helps it spread faster. You can see the *New York Times* in there and the *Washington Post* and then you can see how there's a vast, vast network surrounding and actually choking the mainstream news ecosystem.

The Guardian reports that Albright found 23,000 pages and 1.3 million hyperlinks. And the constellation of websites that he found has another function. More than just spreading fake news and rightwing ideology, they are being used to effectively spread propaganda to track and monitor and influence anyone who comes across their content. Albright said:

> ... I was absolutely dumbfounded. Every time someone

likes one of these posts on Facebook or visits one of these websites, the scripts are then following you around the web. And this enables data-mining and influencing companies like Cambridge Analytica to precisely target individuals, to follow them around the web, and to send them highly personalised political messages. This is a propaganda machine. It's targeting people individually to recruit them to an idea. It's a level of social engineering that I've never seen before. They're capturing people and then keeping them on an emotional leash and never letting them go.

The Guardian also reported that Cambridge Analytica "claims to have built psychological profiles using 5,000 separate pieces of data on 220 million American voters. It knows their quirks and nuances and daily habits and can target them individually."

Steve Bannon, former Breitbart News' executive chairman and, since mid-2016 Donald Trump's chief strategist, sits on the board for Cambridge Analytica.[79] According to the *Motherboard* report, Cambridge Analytica was hired in June, 2016 by the Trump team to provide "dark advertising" that would sway undecided people toward a Trump vote. Cambridge Analytica was able to access this data to search for specific profiles: "all anxious fathers, all angry introverts, for example – or maybe even all undecided Democrats."

"We are thrilled that our revolutionary approach to data-driven communication has played such an integral part in President-elect Trump's extraordinary win," Nix was quoted as saying. According to the *Motherboard* report, "His company wasn't just integral to Trump's online campaign, but to the UK's Brexit campaign as well." In Nix's own words, it worked like this: "At Cambridge," he said, "we were able to form a model to predict the personality of every single adult in the United States of America."

Although Cambridge Analytica apparently denies using Facebook data, psychometrics, and Kosinski's methodology, the *Motherboard* report continues:

> According to Nix, the success of Cambridge Analytica's marketing is based on a combination of three elements: behavioral science using the OCEAN model, Big Data analysis, and ad targeting. Ad targeting is personalized advertising, aligned as accurately as possible to the personality of an individual consumer.

Then these same consumers receive "dark posts", or advertisements specifically devised for them that cannot be viewed by anyone else other than that person.

The *Motherboard* report concludes with this:

> The world has been turned upside down. Great Britain is leaving the EU, and Donald Trump is president of the United States of America. And in Stanford, Kosinski, who wanted to warn against the danger of using psychological targeting in a political setting, is once again receiving accusatory emails. "No," says Kosinski, quietly and shaking his head. "This is not my fault. I did not build the bomb. I only showed that it exists."

Where did the Big Five Theory come from?

The personality theory that lies at the heart of the election-tipping debate, and the source for Kosinski's work, originates with psychometrics, and notably the work of Dr. Raymond Cattell,[80] one of the original "personality test" scholars. Cattell is regaled in Western culture for his contributions to the field of intelligence assessment (IQ and personality work). Despite his direct and profound relationship to the eugenics movement and his recognition by the Nazi Party for the birth of The Beyondists,[81] his work is benignly promoted in scholarly circles. But the fact that he is professionally legitimized does not make him any less the racist he was.[82] And his contributions toward racist practices live on. He has two notable theories of personality development and measurement entitled "The Big Five Theory" and the "Sixteen Personality Factor Questionnaire."

The way that OCEAN's Five Factors personality data from our students can be used

The recent trend toward a "grit narrative," hailed by Angela Duckworth and others, has been gobbled up by school districts around the country. The OCEAN model is used widely by schools and other institutions internationally, and the grit measure has been compared to the Big Five personality model. In addition, there is a growing emphasis on the "affective" learning of students. Some examples include:[83]

> "… recent work done with ETS' SuccessNavigator assessment and ACT's Engage College Domains and Scales Overview … the broader domains in these models are tied to those areas of the big-five personality theory …"

In an "extractive model" for education (one which mines children as a commodity for profit) the personality "profile" of a child – determined by using models such as MacCann's "Facets of Conscientiousness"[84] or OCEAN's Five Factors – becomes a unit of measurement by which financial entities can determine the "risk" in the profitability or return on their investment in that child's education. In the traditional public school model, such predictions are far more diffuse or indirect in terms of financial investment, because tax payer dollars are distributed generally across the state and local populations of that public school system. But in a privatized-for-profit model, where educational services are dependent on private investment (corporate and philanthropic dollars), then the "investment/risk" model matters a great deal because children are now a form of profit (or loss).

Behavioral predictions are promoted through catchy language such as "grit and tenacity." Grit represents the language for the modern day "plantation" framework which sees children (read: poor children of color) as profit. The "Facets of Conscientiousness" measure determines how profitable a child's future labor may be using the language of capital and output to describe learners' personality profiles, highlighting the values of "Orderliness, Industriousness, and Control" [65]

While "grit" has been exposed for the racist narrative it is,[85] it's also a direct by-product of the same OCEAN framework used to control, predict and manipulate voters. If this data can sway major national elections and change the global trajectory of history, imagine the information that such data, gathered on children, day after day, year after year, could yield for corporations and government interests. The U.S. Dept of Education, Office of Technology 2013 report "Promoting Grit, Tenacity, and Perseverance: Critical Factors for Success in the 21st Century" says so plainly:[86]

> Several private foundations have recently initiated programs to push the frontiers of theory, measurement, and practice around these and related factors, particularly for at-risk and vulnerable students. In national policy, there is increasing attention on 21st-century competencies (which encompass a range of non-cognitive factors, including grit), and *persistence*... (and) the new and emerging roles technologies can play in this paradigm shift.

Watch the video[87] from Jesse Schell, gaming CEO, to see exactly where this can go. As Schell says in another video[88] "your shopping data is a goldmine and it's only a matter of time before gaming companies and gaming behavior interface with our daily consumer and behavioral choices. You can get points for simply brushing your teeth long enough when product brands partner with gaming systems."

We now have, thanks to perpetual assessments of children's knowledge affective "grit" or personality, "the concept of the 'preemptive personality,' the endlessly profiled and guided subject who is shunted into recalculated futures in a system that could be characterized as digital predestination".[89]

The role of education technology (aka "personalized learning")

According to a report entitled "Networks of Control":[90]

Jennifer Whitson (2013) argues that today's technology-based practices of gamification are "rooted in surveillance" because they provide "real-time feedback about users' actions by amassing large quantities of data". According to her, gamification is "reliant on quantification", on "monitoring users' everyday lives to measure and quantify their activities". **Gamification practices based on data collection and quantification** are "leveraging surveillance to evoke behavior change" … While **self-quantification** promises to "make daily practices more fulfilling and fun" by adopting "incentivization and pleasure rather than risk and fear to shape desired behaviours", it also became "a new driving logic in the technological expansion and **public acceptance of surveillance**". [emphasis in original]

The schools of the future promise to track and record your every emotion no matter how hard you try to hide it. For example, an online conference for technology companies in February 2016 called "The Pearson CITE Online Learning Conference"[91] highlighted a pre-conference session[92] entitled "Measuring Learning Impact Using Next Gen Tools: A Learner-Centered View of Learning Affect, Behavior and Cognition" presented by iMotions, Inc. and Pearson Achievement.[93] They claim that "Measuring how a learner's emotions influence final learning outcomes further supports iterative design decisions that can impact learner engagement." Their products include devices for: eye tracking, facial recognition, surveys, scene cameras, and biosensors.

This has been over a decade on the making. In 2000 *Business Week* listed the companies benefiting from the new boon in online education stating, "**Dozens of new companies are springing up** to serve the **emerging K-12 market for digital learning**. Investors have poured nearly $1 billion into these companies since the beginning of 1999, estimates Merrill Lynch."

The "gold" in data mining of future generations, via a private for-profit model of education is not merely in the uses of data collections procedures paid for by taxpayer dollars (i.e. paying Pearson for an online curriculum service). It's about using the data collected to sell children products, to predict social outcomes for them, and to manage their social realities, as in the role of Cambridge Analytica in the 2016 election …not simply selling us products but re-forming our sense of choice, freedom and democracy to suit global corporate interests.

Connect the Dots

Corporate and state control of public education no longer provides viable options that benefit the average human being (the 99%). We must re-imagine ways to provide public services as a common good. As Naomi Klein says in her 2014 book *This Changes Everything*:[94]

> All of this is why any attempt to rise to the climate challenge [*I would add, education challenge*] will be fruitless unless it is understood as part of a much broader battle of world views, a process of rebuilding and reinventing the very idea of the collective, the communal, the commons, the civil, and the civic after so many decades of attack and neglect. (p. 460).

The Trump administration is placing so many health and human services on the chopping block – environment (EPA), labor (unions) and education (children) are all soon to be sold to corporate interests. The appointment of Betsy DeVos to U.S. Secretary of Education did not instigate this take-over, but she will certainly expedite the process. We need to reach beyond our silos and work together across issues. Also we must realize that we are connected to each other. Many of us might still enjoy good quality public schools, but we should care nonetheless. We must start caring about others because the pillaging usually reserved only for the marginalized and economically disenfranchised (i.e. closing schools in NOLA) is coming home to roost in increasingly privileged communities and schools. This affects ALL of us.

Too often, we rely on others to change things. We appeal to our legislators. We advocate for piecemeal adjustments to existing laws and tell ourselves compromise is necessary, that change is slow, and that we can't expect too much. Within the existing power structure those statements would be/are true.

But it's time to dismantle these power-infrastructures.

The current battle (moving forward) will demand a totally

revolutionary dismantling of existing social, political, economic and power structures, in which asking "mother may I" of our politicians and education leaders will not suffice. The movement must mobilize from the bottom up, at localized levels, with rhizomatic power structures rather than hierarchical ones, in which compassion and care for others as well as ourselves, all matter. The work is co-operative, collaborative, and democratic. It will NOT be led by corporate funded sponsors like Cambridge Analytica using psy ops to predict and control our choices, and the futures of our children.

Why do we force children to sit at computers all day keying in data even though we know it will lead to increase in all sorts of learning, developmental, and social problem? Why do we administer meaningless tests that bring children to tears? Somewhere along the lines we forgot about our OWN power. **Reclaim it.**

An earlier version of this chapter was originally published under the same title on the author's "Educationalchemy" blog in February 2017

TRUMP SAYS OUR SCHOOLS ARE "FLUSH WITH CASH!?" THEY'RE FALLING APART!

STEVEN SINGER

Steven Singer is a Public School Teacher, Education Advocate and Author of the "Gadfly on the Wall" Blog

Our schools have not gotten worse; they've stayed the same.

Donald Trump lies.

If you haven't learned that yet, America, you've got four more cringe-inducing years to do so.

Even in his inaugural address,[95] he couldn't help but let loose a whooper about US public schools.

"Americans want great schools for their children, safe neighborhoods for their families and good jobs for themselves," he said. "But for too many of our citizens, a different reality exists. … An education system flush with cash but which leaves our young and beautiful students deprived of all knowledge."

To which nearly every poor, nonwhite public school parent, student and teacher in the country replied, "What the heck did he just say now!?"

Los Angeles Unified School District[96] routinely has broken desks and chairs, missing ceiling tiles, damaged flooring, broken sprinklers, damaged lunch tables and broken toilet paper dispensers.

They're flush with cash!?

New York City public schools[97] removed more than 160 toxic light fixtures containing polychlorinated biphenyls, a cancer causing agent that also hinders cognitive and neurological development. Yet many schools are still waiting on a fix, especially those serving minority students.

They're flush with cash!?

At Charles L. Spain School in Detroit,[98] the air vents are so warped and moldy, turning on the heat brings a rancid stench. Water drips from a leaky roof into the gym, warping the floor tiles. Cockroaches literally scurry around some children's classrooms until they are squashed by student volunteers.

They're flush with freakin cash!?

Are you serious, Donald Trump!?

And this same picture is repeated at thousands of public schools across the nation especially in impoverished neighborhoods. Especially in communities serving a disproportionate number of black, Latino or other minority students.

In predominantly white, upper-class neighborhoods, the schools often **ARE** "flush with cash." Olympic-size swimming pools, pristine bathrooms – heck – air conditioning! But in another

America across the tracks, schools are defunded, ignored and left to rot.

A full 35 states provide less overall state funding for education today than they did in 2008, according to the Center on Budget and Policy Priorities,[99] which focuses on reducing poverty and inequality. Most states still haven't recovered from George W. Bush's Great Recession and the subsequent state and local budget cuts it caused. In fact, over the same period, per pupil funding fell in 27 states and still hasn't recovered.

And the federal government has done little to help alleviate the situation. Since 2011, spending on major K-12 programs[99] – including Title I grants for underprivileged students and special education – has been basically flat.

The problem is further exacerbated by the incredibly back-ward way we allocate funding[100] at the local level, which bears the majority of the cost of education.

While most advanced countries divide their school dollars evenly between students, the United States does not. Some students get more, some get less. It all depends on local wealth.[101]

The average per-pupil expenditure for US secondary students is $12,731.[102] But that figure is deceiving. It is an average. Some kids get much more. Many get much less. It all depends on where you live. If your home is in a rich neighborhood, more money is spent on your education than if you live in a poor neighborhood.

The US is one of the only countries in the world – if not probably the **ONLY** country – that funds schools based largely on local taxes.[103] Other developed nations either equalize funding or provide extra money for kids in need. In the Netherlands,[104] for example, national funding is provided to all schools based on the number of pupils enrolled. But for every guilder allocated to a middle-class Dutch child, 1.25 guilders are allocated for a lower-class child and 1.9 guilders for a minority child – exactly the opposite of the situation in the US

So, no. Our schools are not "flush with cash." Just the opposite in many cases.

But what about Trump's other claim – the much-touted narrative of failing schools?

Trump says our schools "leave… our young and beautiful students deprived of all knowledge."

Not true.

Graduation rates are at an all-time high of 83.2 percent.[105] Moreover, for the first time minority students are catching up with their white counterparts.

It's only international comparisons of standardized test scores that support this popular myth of academic failure. And, frankly, even that is based on a warped and unfair reading of those results.

It depends on how you interpret the data.

Raw data shows US children far from the top of the scale. It puts us somewhere in the middle[106] – where we've always been for all the decades since they've been making these comparisons. Our schools have not gotten worse. They have stayed the same.[107]

However, this ignores a critical factor – poverty. We've known for decades that standardized tests are poor measures of academic success.[108] Bubble tests can assess simple things but nothing complex. After all, they're scored based on answers to multiple choice questions. In fact, the only thing they seem to measure with any degree of accuracy is the parental income of the test-taker.[109] Kids from rich families score well, and poor kids score badly.

Virtually all of the top-scoring countries taking these exams have much less child poverty than the US.[110] If they had the same percentage of poor students that we do, their scores would be lower than ours. Likewise, if we had the same percentage of poor students that they do, our scores would go through the roof! We would have the best scores in the world!

Moreover, the US education system does something that many international systems do not. We educate everyone! Foreign systems often weed children out by high school.[111] They don't let every child get 13 years of grade school (counting kindergarten). They only school their highest achievers.

So when we compare ourselves to these countries, we're comparing ALL of our students to only **SOME** of theirs – their best academic pupils, to be exact. Yet we still hold our own given these handicaps!

This suggests that the majority of problems with our public schools aren't bad teachers, or a lack of charter schools and school choice. It's money, pure and simple.

We invest the majority of our education funding in rich white kids. The poor and minorities are left to fend for themselves.

This won't be solved by Trump's pick for education secretary, Betsy DeVos[112] and her school-choice schemes. In fact, that's exactly what's weakened public schools across the country by leaching away what meager funding these districts have left. Nor will it be solved by a demagogue telling fairy tales to Washington's credulous and ignorant.

We need to make a real investment in our public schools. We need to make a commitment to funding poor black kids as fairly as we do rich white kids.

Otherwise, the only thing flushed will be children's future.

This chapter was originally published under the same title on the author's "Gadfly on the Wall" blog in January 2017

THE RACIST GENIE IS OUT OF THE BOTTLE (AGAIN): A STUDENT-TEACHER DISCUSSION

RUSS WALSH

Russ Walsh is a Public School Teacher, Literacy Specialist, Curriculum Supervisor and College Instructor, and Author of "A Parent's Guide to Public Education" (Garn Press) And the "Russ on Reading" Blog

Like many teachers across the country, I walked into my classroom for the first time after the election with a sense of trepidation. I teach a college freshman class focused on reading improvement. The class is quite diverse, about 55% African-American, 30% white, and 15% Hispanic. I planned to address the election because I knew it would be on the mind of all my students. I planned to show them the video of President Obama's post-election speech from the White House lawn. The President, following the tradition of Presidents before him, sought to ensure a smooth transition and articulated a hope that all American citizens would work together

89

for the success of a Trump presidency. I told the students that the President was trying to show us the best way to respond to surprising and perhaps worrying change.

I then asked the students to write in their interactive notebooks in response to this prompt: What are some of your worries and some of your hopes as we look forward to a Trump presidency? The students wrote for about 15 minutes and then I invited them to share. More hands went up than at any other time in the semester. Worries, for the most part followed a familiar pattern. Students of Hispanic descent cited fear that they or their friends and relatives would be targeted for deportation. Some students worried about the hateful targeting of their Muslim, Hispanic, and African-American friends. Many students expressed surprise that so many women had voted for Trump in the wake of his sexist statements and behavior. One student worried that the election would further divide the country, while another student offered that he thought the campaign had divided the country long before the election took place and he blamed both candidates for taking the low road. The students were thoughtful and articulate and impassioned.

One student offered the hope that Trump would moderate his attacks on people of color, Muslims, immigrants and others now that he had won the election and realized he had to serve all of us. I said I thought we could all agree that this was greatly to be hoped.

And then it happened. Something I was not expecting, but something that brought great clarity to what this election really means to many of the young people in my classroom.

A normally quiet young woman raised her hand and said, "It is not so much Trump I am worried about, but his followers who now feel free to act out all their feelings towards minorities." The young woman then went on to tell about three separate incidents of intimidation and bias that had been directed at her, on campus, to her face, since the election. The young woman, who is Hispanic and born in this country, was asked if she was ready to be deported now that Trump was elected. Other taunts of the "we are going to build that wall and send you back where you came from" variety came a little later and she reported them to campus authorities, all of them written down on her phone so she could get the language verbatim.

Another young woman raised her hand to report on a tweet she received that stated, "If my president can grab your pussy, then I can, too." Other young women reported receiving the same tweet. Another student reported on a tweet she received saying that, "At last we won't have to put up with those 'things' coming over the border, cause Trump is going to build a wall." Several students reported on racist tweets that were circulating since the election. Another student said that friends reported to her that they had voted for Trump because every time they saw a Muslim on the street they were afraid and Trump was going to kick them out.

Trump's campaign of hate has let the genie out of the bottle. The racism that is never far from the surface in America has been unleashed, has been made acceptable and has empowered the most bigoted in our society to own their bigotry as a weapon against all people they identify as the "other." I talked briefly, trying to give all this context, about Germany in the 1930s and how the politics of fear can unleash the most horrific perversions of human behavior.

A young man raised his hand. "I am scared, and all my friends in the LGBT community are scared, too. We don't know much about Trump's position on LGBT rights, but we know all about his Vice President, Mike Pence's, positions on gays and transgender people. I fear that since Trump doesn't have any experience in governing, he will listen to people like Mike Pence." The emotion in the young man's voice was palpable. His classmates offered support, and I lost it.

"Look folks," I said. "This is not OK. You need to know that this is not OK. If any of you at any time are subject to any of these attacks, tweets, Facebook posts or just campus innuendo either because of your race, your gender, your sexual identity, please report what has happened immediately. If you are afraid to report it to the authorities on campus, come to me and we will do it together. This must stop now."

It was a highly emotional classroom. We never got to the planned essay reading for the day. Class ended in hugs and attempted reassurance. When I got home and shared with my wife, she told me about news reports coming in from around the country of similar types of intimidation and race baiting in schools and public places.

This morning the New York Times published an editorial[113] asking that the President-elect directly and immediately denounce the hate and let his supporters know that this targeting behavior is not OK. But once you let the hate genie out of the bottle, it is devilishly difficult to put it back in. Racism, xenophobia, and misogyny are never far from the surface in this country and when these baser instincts of humans seem to have the imprimatur of the leader of the country, it may take a lifetime to tame them.

As teachers, we need to be on guard and vigilant. We must re-double our efforts to make sure the classroom, the hallways, the cafeteria, the locker room, the campus are safe for all people, including Trump supporters, who will almost certainly be the targets of backlash as well.

In 1992, Rodney King, the African-American victim of a brutal police beating in Los Angeles asked, "Can we all get along?" Apparently not, Rodney. Not yet, anyway. There is still a lot of work to be done.

This chapter was originally published on the author's "Russ On Reading" blog in November 2016.

DIGNITY FOR MY MUSLIM STUDENTS AND THEIR FAMILIES

KATIE LAPHAM

Katie Lapham is a NYC Public School Teacher and Author of the "Critical Classrooms, Critical Kids" Blog

The majority of U.S. citizens do not support the current predator-in-chief.* He does not speak for us or represent our views. With every ounce of energy we can summon from our weary bodies (and souls), we vehemently condemn Donald Trump. Almost daily, protests against Trump and his inner circle take place around the world. In our free time we make signs, call our government representatives, send postcards, and attend rallies all in resistance to the new administration. Here in New York City, we also scrub off swastikas and other hate messages scrawled on playground equipment and subway trains. As an English as a Second Language (ESL) teacher in Brooklyn, I'm particularly outraged by Trump's Muslim ban, which temporarily bars citizens – including refugees – of Iraq, Libya, Somalia, Sudan, Syria, Yemen and Iran from entering the United States.

For the past seven years, I have had the privilege of working with English-language learners from Yemen and Sudan, two of the countries included in the Muslim ban. Their families are not terrorists. They are not a national security threat. In fact, the CATO Institute recently reported that "Foreigners from those seven nations have killed zero Americans in terrorist attacks on U.S. soil between 1975 and the end of 2015." My current students – aged five to eleven – trade Pokémon cards and read Diary of a Wimpy Kid. They are artists, writers and mathematicians. My Muslim students play soccer and make drawings of purple horses and flowers. They cry when they fall on the ice and bleed. Last year, one student broke my heart when she regularly interrupted me to tell me that her cousins in Yemen had no food and were starving. And in November, a truly perplexed fourth grader asked me, "Why does Trump think we are terrorists?"

While the horrors in Syria have been widely reported, and rightly so, mainstream media barely makes a peep about the bloodshed in Yemen. According to UNICEF, one child dies every 10 minutes in Yemen. Children there are severely malnourished and lack access to clean water, food and medical care. This is due – in large part – to a civil war that has been raging in Yemen since 2015. Not surprisingly, the United States has been involved in the conflict as an arms supplier to the Saudi Arabia-led coalition, which through its attacks on Houthi rebels, has indiscriminately murdered thousands of Yemeni civilians, including children. Zaid Jilani, in his January 25, 2017 article in *The Intercept*, said Trump's Muslim immigration executive order is "...like a twisted version of the you-break-it-you-buy-it Pottery Barn rule: If we bomb a country or help destabilize its society, we will then ban its citizens from being able to seek refuge in the United States."

Regarding Sudan, we all have heard about the atrocities that have taken place in Darfur since 2003. According to the United Nations, the genocide in Darfur has contributed greatly to the displacement of an estimated 3.5 million people in Sudan. Much less known though is Jebel Marra in Darfur province, which since 2004 has also been under violent attack by President Omar al-Bashir. Amnesty International has compelling evidence showing that in 2016 alone, 30 attacks involving chemical weapons have occurred in Jebel Marra. Amnesty's Director of Crisis Response, Tirana Hassan, paints a grim picture of the aftermath of these attacks by noting, "...babies screaming with pain before dying, young children vomiting blood. The images we have seen are truly shocking." Food insecurity, lack of medical care, a raging civil war in South Sudan, among other barbarities, have also befallen Sudanese civilians.

If we Americans were living in such circumstances, wouldn't we want to be afforded the opportunity to resettle in a more stable and open society, perhaps to reunite with family members? Here in the United States, we have a strong tradition of welcoming immigrants and refugees, and of fighting intolerance and injustice. Beginning with the Quakers, Amish and Huguenots in the late 1600s, the city of Lancaster, Pennsylvania, for example, has had a long tradition of opening its community to refugees, including recent arrivals from Sudan, Somalia and Iraq. Immigrants and refugees enrich our lives. For Trump to close our nation's doors to them is un-American. It is not who we are.

As the school year progresses, my Muslim students may want to discuss recent events with me. The older ones may wonder why their countries were singled out. I may have to explain to them why Saudi Arabia, Egypt and UAE – countries producing a large number of anti-American terrorists, including those behind 9/11 – were not listed in Trump's Muslim ban, and why they are U.S. allies while the U.S. simultaneously bombs or imposes sanctions on Iraq, Libya, Somalia, Sudan, Syria, Yemen and Iran. How many people know that this was happening under President Obama? Or perhaps my students will just want to tell me about Pokèmon trainers. Whatever awaits me, I will continue to rage inside against this grave injustice. My newcomer kindergartener will reach for my hand, as she always does, and I will think about how lucky she is to have arrived here before 2017. I will continue to wonder about the safety and well-being of her relatives in Yemen while – through gestures and individual words – she tells me the names of the shapes she's learned and asks to borrow one of my books. The humanity I experience in my school on a daily basis is comforting, and, I believe, reflects the decency and compassion of most U.S. citizens. Observing my students – Muslim, Hispanic, Jewish, Black, White – all being kids together is, for me, the greatest joy of teaching.

Trump's actions and rhetoric, on the other hand, are vile and inhumane. He must be stopped, for as we are witnessing, he is an impediment to our ability to become a more tolerant, democratic and caring society. Trump appears to want the opposite and will lie to get it. I vow to protect all of my English-language learners as best I can. During the school day, I will read picture books featuring Muslim children and refugees, and I will stay informed so that I can address any questions or concerns my students may have. I will also uphold NYC Chancellor Carmen Fariña's policy on immigration as outlined in her January 30, 2017 letter to parents. I will not inquire about anyone's immigration status, and any information I know about my students and their families will remain confidential. I will not grant unlimited access to Immigration and Customs Enforcement (ICE). In addition to referring our immigrant families to public services – ActionNYC and the Mayor's Office of Immigrant Affairs – Chancellor Fariña's letter included a message of solidarity. An immigrant herself, Fariña wrote, "We take pride in our diversity. Immigrant parents, students, principals, teachers and other staff are a part of what makes our schools, and New York City, the amazing, strong, vibrant places they are. Whether you or your family arrived 100 years or 100 days ago – you are New Yorkers – and we stand with you." I echo her sentiments.

Outside of school, I will continue to attend rallies and speak out against the racist and xenophobic rhetoric seeping from the Oval Office like clouds of toxic green air. On February 2, I joined thousands of Yemeni-Americans at Brooklyn's Borough Hall to peacefully protest Trump's Muslim ban and to stand in solidarity with the hundreds of Yemeni deli owners who closed their stores for eight hours that day. On a piece of cardboard, I wrote I love my Yemeni bodega** and my Yemeni students. I printed out an image of the Arabic spelling of love and glued it to my poster. Yemeni men and women – some draped in flags representing both the US and Yemen – asked to take a picture with me. "Thank you," they said to me while clutching their hearts and smiling. I want the Muslim community to know that unlike Donald Trump, I value their lives. I don't see myself or any other immigrant group as better than they are. Working with my Muslim students has helped me to grow not just as an educator but also as a human being. I will resist Trump always.

* I am crediting Winona LaDuke for this term.
** bodega is a term used in NYC when referring to a deli or small corner grocery store.

EMPATHY, DIVERSITY, AND BEING "MEAN TO ALL PEOPLE": THE DEMOCRATIC WORK OF THE PUBLIC'S SCHOOLS IN HARD TIMES

ANNE HAAS DYSON

Anne Haas Dyson is Professor of Education, a Recipient of the NCTE Outstanding Educator of the Year Award, and Author of "Negotiating a Permeable Curriculum" (Garn Press)

"If Donald Trump wins, I'm moving to Canada," said Ta'Von, a 7-year old child I have known since he was in preschool. It was the spring of 2016, and Donald Trump was closing in on the Republican nomination. No doubt having participated in family talk on the election, Ta'Von had decided that "I'm not having Donald Trump as my president. The only presidents I would stay for is Hilary Clinton or you." (blush)

Ta'Von is proud of his African American heritage. He is an

avid student of history, favorite topics being Black leaders and U.S. Presidents, especially Barak Obama, John F. Kennedy, and Abraham Lincoln. He rejected Donald Trump as president because, unlike those he most admired, Trump "is mean to all people." Mean to all people.

This meanness pervaded Trump's loud, unrelenting rhetoric of divisiveness and dismissal. That rhetoric singled out as "other" one segment of society and then another. Economic struggles and life disappointments of "white" workers (and those out of work) were not caused by new economic and social dynamics but by those deemed outsiders. "They" caused "us" problems. "They" live in crime-infested neighborhoods, did not work, and took "our" tax money. Then there were those who came into the country without papers and cut in line in front of "us" to get jobs (Hochschild, 2016).[114]

Like Ta'Von, children all over the country were listening to this discourse (Bazelon, 2016; Costello, 2016).[115] [116] In that talk, children's presence was not noted, their sense of safety was of no concern, nor was the bullying of children targeted by taunts from those feeling privileged. Herein, with the help of Ta'Von, I consider the nature of this "mean" discourse, including its lack of empathy and its neoliberal roots. In the context of such discourse, we might turn with a sense of urgency to the potential of our public's schools; there, in schools that serve all who come to the door, we may find teachers and children too whose actions remind us of our interconnectedness and our need for empathetic but critical participation in a shared life.

I begin, then, by introducing my current companion in a public school (and in this essay), Ta'Von, a small child with a huge sense of democratic inclusiveness.

Ta'Von: Hope Grounded in the Everyday

I first met Ta'Von in his beloved preschool, which served a racially and linguistically diverse group of children, primarily from low-income homes. I then went along with him as he transitioned to his current school, which serves primarily majority children in a neighborhood of economic and social privilege.

Beginning from his first day in kindergarten, he was clearly "the other," with his braided hair ("girl" hair to certain peers), his lack of a water bottle (the unwritten material requirement of neighborhood children), and his perceived need for, and inability to proffer, help (the view of neighborhood kids labeled "bright"). Despite this othering, Ta'Von remained dignified and proud in his racial identity. (He colored himself brown and added braids to every picture he drew that included him.) And he expressed audible pleasure when he accomplished a task ("I did it!") or someone who he knew had been struggling achieved success ("You did it!"), both echoes of his preschool culture.

Moreover, throughout the primary grades, Ta'Von maintained his social outgoingness and his desire to be friends with all people. In this essay, I draw on small everyday moments from his primary years, using them as counter-narratives to the divisive rhetoric that surrounds us. It is those moments that sustain me and, perhaps, other educators in the midst of the hateful rhetoric of our times. And so we begin below with empathy.

Empathy and the Construction of the Common Good

I sit down beside second-grader Ta'Von one day, and he wonders if I have brought him a promised book on a blues guitarist, blues and jazz being another great interest of his. "I'm not very good at patience," he says, perhaps rethinking his greeting.

I did bring it, I explain, but I would give it to him at recess, so he could put it in his back pack to take home. "I don't have a book for everyone," I say, and "I don't want kids to feel bad."

"Oh," he says. "But what if you did [have a book for everybody]? They'd be so happy!"

That response, oriented to others' joy, was vintage Ta'Von. The emergence of such empathetic responses is visible in the very first year of life (Roth-Hanania, Davidov, & Zahn-Waxler, 2011).[117] Our humanity, our culture, our language, our very survival depend on being able to feel along with others. Around age two, when we are more mobile and agile, we may act on our empathy, reaching out to comfort whoever seems in distress. However, in the course of growing up, we may learn that some are "us" and some are "them," not worthy of our empathy and our respect for their humanity.

What, then, are we as teachers to make of the divisive rhetoric that characterized Trump's candidacy and now his presidency – the name-calling, the insults, the disparagement of whole groups of people? In schools, such behavior, if habitual, would lead to a phone call home to a caregiver and an action plan for change.

Moreover, what are our children making of it? Ta'Von was not the only child watching as American people were meanly splintered – the "Mexicans," the disabled, the African Americans in disrespected neighborhoods, the tossed aside Islamic citizens, including the grieving parents of a felled soldier, and the women who, as physical objects, did not "impress" him (an out-of-shape old man). Panic set in among many children who were part of the dismissed, the rejected, and, potentially, the bullied (Bazelon, 2016).[115] The political discourse left us wondering, along with Ta-Nehisi Coates (2015),[118] who exactly is included when politicians invoke "the American people"?

Perhaps the discourse struck the most fear locally among children with roots in Mexico. Sandra Osorio[119] worked with a new teacher, Natalia, in a dual-language (Spanish-English) second grade. Their children too had been listening to, and hearing about, the divisive "mean" election talk, particularly the insults directed to Mexican immigrants and the promises (now acts) of deportation. Many worried that beloved family members would be yanked from their lives because they did not have "papers."

The teachers responded to their children's talk by inviting then to discuss, write, and draw their opinions. One student's letter to Mr. Trump (translated from the original Spanish by Osario[119]) asked, "What if you were separated from a friend, would you like if you were a baby and they take your mom away from you?" In other words, Mr. Trump, do you have no empathy?

The current political climate underscores the importance of our efforts as teachers to build on humanity's empathetic bent, modeling, monitoring, and guiding children to engage in respectful dialogue with each other. We may not think of this as political work, but it is. Empathy, after all, is basic to democracy in a complex society composed of many communities, potentially divided by constructed boundaries of race, religion, social class, and on and on. Participants in society must recognize potential "others" as having life stories propelled by hopes, dreams, and realities and, moreover, as having human rights; all are, therefore, collaborators and companions in negotiating the common good (Baltodano, 2012; Nussbaum, 2016).[120] [121]

Neoliberalism vs. Democratic Participation in Schools

It is December in Ta'Von's kindergarten. His teacher has just read the class a book about how families celebrate holidays differently around the world (but not within their own class). She has asked the children to draw their family getting ready for a holiday. Ta'Von is sitting with Vida, an Iranian immigrant, Nia, who is mixed race (White and African American), and Jacoury (African American); all the children are, in one way or another, "minorities" in this majority white, monolingual school. As I sit down, Vida declares:

Vida: I celebrate Nowruz [traditional Iranian festival].

Jacoury: You can't celebrate naughty.

Nia: She has naughty-hood.

Ta'Von: (firmly) We're not talking about naughty.

Vida: We're not talking about naughty-hood.

Ta'Von is there for Vida. The "naughty" talk stops and, as the interaction continues, the assignment is recalled, the claimed holidays restated, and Ta'Von again mediates relations among Vida, Nia, and himself.

Nia: Ta'Von, what are we suppose' to do again?

Ta'Von: We're suppose' to draw a holiday that we celebrate and get ready for…. I'm doing birthdays.

Nia: I celebrate Christmas.

Vida: I celebrate birthdays.

Ta'Von   I celebrate birthdays too!

Nia: Put me in the picture because I'm gonna have a birthday…

Ta'Von: I celebrate birthdays AND Christmas.

Soon all are drawing; and they are telling stories, as they crawl into their pictures – eating, dancing, and, in Ta'Von's case, cowering in fear as a huge present slips off a table headed right toward his head!

Ta'Von and his tablemates were negotiating an inclusive space. A cultural divide did appear. But the children had more in common than different; all had special times for celebration, when family gathered around a table with special foods and gaiety prevailed (except if a present falls on your head). This experience of negotiating across differences, and Ta'Von's and Vida's insistent demand for respect, contains lessons of democratic participation. But such lessons, like young children's social learning and imaginative play, are devalued now (Genishi & Dyson, 2009).[122]

In the dominant neoliberal discourse, society's members are competitors for the economic avenues to the good life, however it is defined. And freedom, freedom has to do with participation in a choice-filled market (Baltodano, 2012; Volk, 2016).[120][123] Shopping in a superstore, then, is, I suppose, freedom, a freedom predicated on economic success. In this neoliberal rhetoric, the democratic institution of the public's school is just a choice, and not a favored one, as schools for sale are found on a shelf in the marketplace. Moreover, individual achievement, measured on standardized tests, is the gauge for measuring the worth of a chosen school and the "brightness" of a child (Dyson, 2015).[124] Notions of learning to participate in, and help form, a classroom of critical citizenship, as envisioned by Dewey (1916),[125] seem disappeared.

And yet, there was in the above vignette the inevitable need of children themselves for companionship, for empathetic understanding, and for opportunities to produce a meaning-filled life. It is through dialogue, and engagement in play and with the arts, that our freedom as a people is sustained and furthered, so argued Maxine Greene throughout her long career (e.g., Greene, 1988).[126] Freedom is not found when one acts alone in a taken-for-granted world. Rather, it is found in dialogue with the complexities of the world, with people, including those brought to us via the arts – people who reveal unexamined spaces between the taken-for-granted and the unheard, the invisible, the discounted. An expanding sense of self and of space for social action is thus revealed. Our worlds expand even as our interconnections with others become tighter.

Raising Voices, Raising Kids

> Dr. Martin Luther King…was a great guy Because he

> Marched with a lot of People and he marched to freedom and he did That Because he wanted to make the [world] Better…. If anyone got in to a fight, he wanted them to settle it with words not hurting people. Thank you Dr. martin luther king for leading us to Freedom. (Ta'Von, 2nd grade)

In this essay, I have joined with others in this volume, raising my voice in opposition to those who would use their power, and in fact their words, to engage in "hurting people." Like Nussbaum (2010, p. 142),[121] I do not want to base education on producing profits and profit-makers; that, she argues, as sole goals, encourages "a greedy obtuseness and a technically trained docility," which threatens democracy itself. Education, woven with threads of dialogue and the arts, furthers:

> … a world that is worth living in, people who are able to see other human beings as full people with thoughts and feelings of their own that deserve respect and empathy, and nations that are able to overcome fear and suspicion in favor of sympathetic and reasoned debate. (Nussbaum,

2010, p. 143) [121]

In these political times, we collectively do what we have done before – we write petitions and sign them, we call our legislators, we march, and some of us, we alternately rage and cry. But educators have a special role in such anti-democratic, cruel times, as we have influence in the political and moral lives of students, including the very young. In the public's schools, valued by locales across our country, one can find teachers doing such work as patriots and compassionate human beings. Their children's (or fellow educators') comments on what proper girls or boys look like, on singular paths to singular kinds of intelligence, on socioeconomic possessions as indices of with-it-ness, on English as the sole language of those who belong--all are humble opportunities for alert teachers to join with children in breaking free of constructed boxes of "race," class, and gender. Such teachers encourage dialogue. And, sometimes, children themselves – like Ta'Von – will prove to be empathetic, critical participants in worlds shared with peers and with those throughout history who have called this country home.

As I imagine Ta'Von's future, I wish for him such classes, ones that build on his empathy and his appreciation of those, like Martin Luther King, who fought for the equality of all people. In such a class his critical awareness would be nurtured as he learns that those presidents he so admires responded to critical voices as they led the nation. To critique is part of being an active citizen.

And so, inspired by Ta'Von, a child responsive to the social world, I have aimed to raise my voice, not simply against wealth-obsessed politicians with severe social myopia, but for a political culture worthy of our children. Onward.

PEACEMAKING AND THE SEARCH FOR HOME IN DARK TIMES

ESTHER SOKOLOV FINE AND VANESSA BARNETT

Esther Sokolov Fine is Professor Emerita of Education, Former Elementary School Teacher in Downtown Public Housing Communities and Alternative Programs, and Author of "Raising Peacemakers" (Garn Press)

Vanessa Barnett is School District Arts Program Coordinator, University Arts Instructor, and Museum Arts Consultant

In the dark times
Will there also be singing?
Yes, there will also be singing.
About the dark times.

Bertolt Brecht

In Canada, we like to think of ourselves as peacemakers and our schools as places to nurture understanding and mutual respect. Canadian teachers try to foster collaboration and raise peacemakers who will become able to contribute to the building of a compassionate and ethical world. Our classrooms are populated by students from many parts of the globe, a large number of them forced to navigate difficult and often traumatic transitions. Immigrant and refugee students need support to find their way as they learn language and gradually come to feel safe and at home in new surroundings. When we bring children together in a classroom, we have to enable them to share, hear, and come to respect one another. Projects such as *Raising Peacemakers*[127] and *Finding Home* [128] make a positive contribution to the lives of students. In this essay, we focus on two projects in Toronto that have helped students find their way to safety, home, and the work of peacemaking.

In the long-term project, *Children as Peacemaker*[129] – funded by the Social Sciences and Humanities Research Council of Canada (SSHRC) – we see students engaged in a process that begins in kindergarten and continues into adulthood. It started as an initiative in one small public alternative school in downtown Toronto in the late 1980s. A formal study by Esther Sokolov Fine followed the students over a period of twenty-three years. In Esther's research children as young as five were taught in formal and informal ways – in Kindergarten and beyond – how to entertain multiple interpretations of events (and stories) and listen respectfully to differing points of view during moments of tension, disagreement and conflict.

Building and re-building creatively and ethically with students as they go through difficult transitions is, and will always be, a critically important responsibility of teachers. The project, *Finding Home: Personal Journeys and Visual Narratives*, was on exhibit in Toronto at the Aga Khan Museum, and a documentary film of the creative process project provides further information.[128] *

Artist Curators, Vanessa Barnett and Elena Soní (both teachers), are immigrant women who have experienced the reality of loss, separation, longing and memories of family left behind, having immigrated to Canada from South Africa and Venezuela (respectively), escaping the climate of oppression and racism in their home countries. Together with the Visual Arts teachers in the two schools, Vanessa and Elena inspired immigrant and refugee students-in-transition to reflect on their past lives as they were moving through present difficulties and imagining possible futures. The sculptures and accompanying text produced by more than 250 students in a high school and a reception school for new Canadians represents examples of their individual, cultural, community and family journeys to next homes.

Alarming policies in the U.S. are seriously disturbing and destabilizing the lives of many immigrants and refugees who risk everything to create new homes for their families and give their children access to public education. In the years following January 2017 students and teachers in the U.S. (and many parts of the world) will be facing far more than the "traditional" obstacles of public schooling that arise from misguided policy, massive cutbacks, charter schools, standardized testing, poorly designed funding formulas, tax evaders, exploiters of the system and looming dystopic futures.

Vanessa and Elena envisioned this project after Justin Trudeau, Prime Minister of Canada, opened the gates for 25,000 Syrians and other new immigrants to come to Canada at the end of 2016. Trudeau's position stands in stark contrast to Donald Trump's anti-Muslim policy, which purports to put America first by "safeguarding" against a so-called influx of terrorists and criminals.

The project has been extremely pertinent to the dark times we are living in, and critical for the young artists in finding their authentic voices along with a newly reached sense of belonging.

In the *Finding Home* exhibit, there are sculptures by students from Syria, Hungary, Bangladesh, Nigeria, Sri Lanka, Afghanistan, Saudi Arabia and more. One especially striking one by a high school boy from Armenia has an accompanying text that reads, "I found home in the art room at school."

Many of the newly arrived Syrian students witnessed the devastation and displacement of families from the destroyed cities in Homs, Aleppo, Daraa. The destruction of family life is everywhere in the Syrian crisis. Families have lost loved ones because of the violence, and refugees have been separated from their families. For many, normal family patterns of life that we take so much for granted – gathering for a meal, parents and children walking together to school and shopping for groceries at the weekend – have been erased.

The teenage students were hungry for any kind of normalcy – listening to music on their iPhones, playing soccer, singing, eating fast food and comfortably hanging out with friends. They found refuge from dark times by creating artwork that gave them opportunities to express and share their stories, hopes and dreams.

As a first step, all the students met at the Aga Khan Museum to explore the galleries and talk about objects that tell stories about memory and place. The museum honors and teaches about Islamic influences and how geography has inspired and determined ways of life in the Muslim world. Significant objects, manuscripts and artifacts motivated participants to reflect on their own cultural knowledge as they related to places where Muslim life has flourished. They thought about how upheaval, war and forced journeys have influenced culture and identity in new unfamiliar destinations.

The provocation, "What Does Finding Home Mean to you?" resulted in 8 by 11 inch structures that became personal metaphors for their ideas and emotions. These micro dwellings are filled with dreams, fantasies, longing and pride: This is how we cooked, this is where we played, this is how we celebrated, this is who I am.

A wide selection of textures and building materials that included wooden dowels, cane, thin metal sheeting, plexiglass, balsa wood, clay, foam-core and corrugated cardboard suggested possibilities for building that reflected each maker's individuality. The arched doorways, tiled roofs, domes and spires told stories about what it means to carry architectural and cultural memory to new homes. Many of the students had experienced temporary homes along their journey, and for many a sense of ephemerality became part of their material expression. The making of a sculpture signifying "home" served as a framework for significant objects from their own personal history: a piece of fabric, a letter, a key, a pair of earrings. A wooden hand manikin with the names of friends from Slovakia written in fine script. A dinner table with a red airplane resting on the table top, because immigration was at the center of the conversation each night as the family ate their meal. A bicycle leaning against a wall in a courtyard in Saudi Arabia. A detailed replica of a metal lock from a house in Pakistan. A photograph of a family's reunification at Pearson Airport in Toronto. A fish curry recipe from a Bengali grandmother. A room in a mud home in Afghanistan complete with a traditional burgundy woven carpet. A thatched reed kubo on a beach in the Philippines. And hundreds more!

The students scanned or took photographs of their significant object and incorporated these images and textures into their pieces. The use of text in first language became an integral element in the development of the structures as words and stories were incorporated through embroidery, digital copying and writing directly onto the structure.

The incentive for the *Finding Home* project was the establishment of a physical, tactile and social community among new Canadian students. While the exhibit can be seen digitally, it was important to exhibit it in a museum and to have created it in the social environment of a classroom where a community grew through shared art and stories.

Adequate funding, a rich array of found materials and inspiring teachers are necessary ingredients for quality arts programming where *all* students have opportunities to discover the potential of materials and learn what it means to weave ideas and make socially relevant art together. Collaboration and community engagement in these moments is central. In the *Finding Home* project, the individual students described their sculptures. Here are a few of their voices.

Siam Islam: "My art work is about emptiness. It relates to the idea of home because it shows that I left my birth place and the place I grew up and came to Canada for a better life and education. I chose wood because it is the material most used in Chittagong, Bangladesh. In Canada I have not seen wooden houses. My project shows my empty room before I left Chittagong with a suitcase beside the empty bed."

Siam Islam's Artwork – Yellow Suitcase In Empty Room

Razmik Nalbandian: "I am Ballroom dancer. When I dance I feel the most alive. When I dance I feel the true me. This is where I feel safe, this is where I feel at home. The shoe represents the state of being alive and spreading the positive energy by dancing. Our world is full of anger and sadness, I try to live from within being positive and expressing myself through art and found a home in the art room making art."

Razmik Nalbandian's Artwork – Blue Boy

Kadija Farooq: "I created two floors – one where I designed a traditional Pakistani home and one that showed a typical Canadian home. In the Canadian home (top floor) I created a bookshelf to showcase my love of books, a decorative vase, a sofa to provide the typical home feeling, a small picture of a half Pakistani and half Canadian flag, and a carpet. In the Pakistani home (below) I created a charpai, a basket of oranges to symbolize my family's orange farm, a traditional stool, and other important objects that are a part of my idea of a Pakistani home. I also added a picture of my family's orange farm as a background. I thought about where my home is right now and what it means to have a home. For me, Canada and Pakistan are both my home."

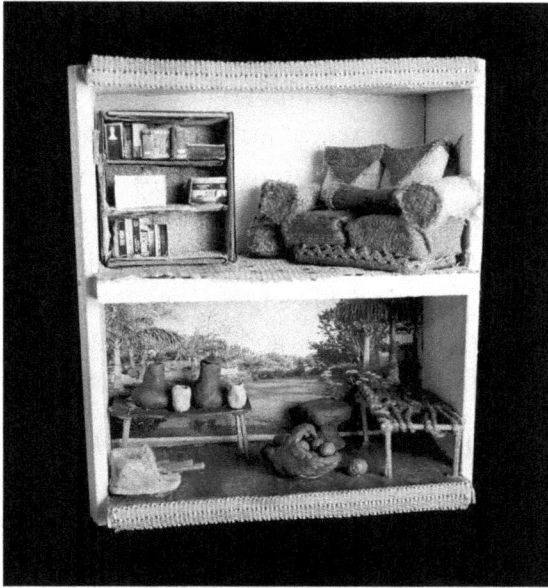

Kadija Farooq's Artwork

The individual dwellings were curated as a long horizontal installation that visually created depths, angles, a feeling of layering and interesting juxtaposition. The curation was further inspired by the imagery of the favelas of Brazil, the corrugated housing in the Zaatari and Azraq camps in Jordan, informal settlements in South Africa and birdhouse structures in Lahore, Pakistan. The assemblages of Alfredo and Isabel Aquilizan, inspired by their relocation from the Philippines to Australia, creating works from re-purposed cardboard to resemble a shanty town perched on a wooden boat, emphasized the precarious concept of home.[130]

Vanessa and Elena were aware that the project had the potential to generate difficult memories, and this was poignantly evident when they arranged to take a group of Syrian students back to the Aga Khan Museum to see the exhibit, *Syria: A Living History*, being shown alongside *Finding Home*. In hindsight, the visit was too immediate, dark and achingly familiar as students confronted images of buildings with facades ripped away, "This could have been my apartment building in Homs" said Adham. In the project's documentary, we see Adham putting the finishing touches to his artwork, a table laden with Syrian delicacies that now seats only two, he describes his recent arrival in Canada. "When I was in Syria, I was living with my parents and my brother. When I left Syria from the war it cost me a lot, that I lost my mother and my father, and now I only live with my brother. I lost everything, and when I came to Canada people support me to find it again. I am really thankful for them and it is good thing that Canadian people care a lot about other countries and about human beings."

During the three months of the *Finding Home* project, the students grew in self-confidence, gained fluency as speakers of English and formed meaningful relationships with one another. They astonished each other with artwork about themselves that was relevant to what they were thinking and feeling, and they were deeply proud to have their work curated and exhibited in a museum. The students' courageous voices depicting their personal journeys and visual narratives have been validated in a landmark exhibition that is current, topical and urgently relevant. How instructive it would be to follow these new Canadian artists into the next phase of their lives as has been done in the long-term peacemaking study.

In a later phase of *Raising Peacemakers* when most of the participants were in high school, videotaped interviews revealed moving and sometimes dark stories about ways in which they were carrying childhood strategies into their more adult lives. One helped others find voice and compassion in a group home where she was living – one as part of a community support organization where she taught and facilitated conflict resolution with teenagers – another who bravely and productively faced peers in a high school where there was a serious problem with bullying – and yet another who worked as a graduate assistant for Stephen Lewis,

Canada's former Ambassador to the United Nations (*Raising Peacemakers*, p. 26).

In this year of huge political change there are high stakes challenges for adults. Let us not forsake our children. If we were to take care of public schools, instead of abandoning or privatizing them, what we could have by 2022 is a model for collaborative, creative learning environments in which all students are creatively engaged in peacemaking and global discussions both in the classroom and in expanded networks in a *lingua franca* of voices. We have the technology, the teachers and the means. What we need is the *will* to open up a wider conversation among many students, some from behind impossibly high walls. We believe that, given the opportunity, all students learn from the tears, the joy, the creative process and from that Brechtian singing about the dark times.

Finding Home: Personal Journeys and Visual Narratives (December 13, 2016 to January 29, 2017) celebrates a socially engaged partnership between the Aga Khan Museum, co-curators Vanessa Barnett and Elena Soní, together with students, teachers and administrators from Greenwood Secondary School and Marc Garneau Collegiate Institute in the Toronto District School Board. This project was supported thorough an Artist in Education grant from the Ontario Arts Council. *Finding Home* reflects the way Canadian students of immigrant parents, newly arrived refugee students and immigrant youth have interpreted the concept of home and what it means to "have a roof over your head."

LEST THERE BE SOME CONFUSION: A PUBLIC EDUCATION BENEFITS EVERYONE

CAROLYN WALKER

Carolyn Walker is a journalist, memoirist, essayist, poet, and creative writing instructor nominated for a Pushcart Prize, and Author of "Every Least Sparrow" (Garn Press)

Some scenes are so arresting that I never forget them. I preserve every detail as if in the past several decades I hadn't stepped away from them, like this one: the creamy yellow cinderblock walls, the pint-sized chairs and tables, the primary-colored decorations, the scent of chalk and floor wax, the children's music: Twinkle, Twinkle Little Star emanating from a record player. A teacher stands next to it, her arms moving like a conductor's. The children, six of them, tap out the beat with drumsticks. Their sticks float like branches on a gentle breeze.

I can still see my daughter, Jennifer, bouncing enthusiastically in a chair, excited by how the world was opening up to her.

She had remarkably good rhythm for a girl who was not quite three years old. Her body was squat and pudgy, her spine shaped like a C. Her stubby legs stuck straight out in front of her, the toes of her white high-top shoes angled away from each other. Her face was rapt in the joy of music, aimed toward the ceiling in what I recognized as toddler ecstasy. A gleeful little tow-head sat next to her. He held his sticks with fingerless hands that were formed into the shape of lobster claws. His face resembled that of a Great White shark, his toothy upper palate jutting impossibly forward, his scant lower jaw in its shadow.

I didn't know it at the moment – I couldn't fathom it, really – but in another fifteen years I would encounter him again. He'd be doing rollouts and stretch kicks in the dojo with my son's karate class. He wouldn't look one bit different, except this time he'd be nearly six feet tall. I watched him execute his moves, and marveled at how nimble and quick he was. Although I was surprised to see him again, this time my impulse wasn't to turn away.

In the years since I'd first encountered Frank I'd seen many disabled people, usually in our local schools or at our community's special summer camp, SCAMP, an outgrowth of our educational system founded by parents and educators, dedicated to disabled children. My daughter grew up actively, and I might add joyously, participating in both scenarios. I had come to understand the importance of interaction – how it benefits everyone – and mourned for the people who were denied this kind of opportunity in previous decades. The federal government's 1975 determination that disabled students were entitled to a free, public education, in the least restrictive environment, was instrumental in bringing folks out of the dark ages and into the light of our modern world.

I think back to what the teacher, Pat, told me when I first saw

Frank on my visit to the elementary classroom that day in 1979.
Four years had passed since the Education for All Handicapped
Children Act (EHA) had been adopted, making the moment pos-
sible.

    "Frank attends school so he'll grow used to the stares of
others," Pat said. I remember that her comment rang around inside
my head like a pinball in an arcade machine. Didn't I stare when I
walked into the classroom? Didn't I embarrass myself in this way?

    Back when my daughter was a bit over two-and-a-half years
old, Pat had brought Jennifer and me to the school by way of
introducing special education opportunities to us. She was keen
on the benefits of what she called "early intervention" – getting a
pro-active jumpstart on a child's learning potential. The class that
Frank attended was designated POHI, she told me, for Physically
or Otherwise Health Impaired students. Children in this classroom
had been gathered from schools throughout the county. Most of
them were between two and four years old, all with similar needs.

    She didn't use these exact words, but I could see that it was a
clustering of students with all sorts of disabilities. Some were only
affected in the body – their arms and legs, or perhaps their eyes, a
little off – and some like my daughter had both physical and mental
challenges. They had attained various levels of accomplishment,
but they were all behind the milestone achievements of children
their age who didn't have disabilities.

    Early intervention, Pat said, would make a difference in Jen-
nifer's outlook, progress and quality of life. She and one of her
associates had come to our home one afternoon and, with tests
disguised as games, had evaluated the best school placement for
my daughter. I had felt both appreciative and encouraged. I was
still getting used to the fact that my child was handicapped. It was
nice to have this hope.

The EHA law, [renamed the Individuals with Disabilities Education Act (IDEA) in 1990], entitles children with disabilities to a public education that begins at birth and carries on into their early twenties. It's meant to help them find their best life and, when necessary, includes physical, speech and occupational therapies.

After Pat left my house, I wished someone would have told me this sooner because my daughter clearly needed this kind of help. She couldn't walk. She could scarcely feed herself. She had a six-word vocabulary. She couldn't use a toilet.

I remember the first time I put her on a yellow school bus, with a baby bottle and a diaper bag. I nervously handed her up to the bus driver who, standing on the top step, hovered over me like an inflated blimp. She held my daughter in her arms and promised she'd take good care of her. I let go. I watched the bus pull away from my driveway, my daughter too small to see out the window. I felt a little lost. A little empty. I pondered what I should do next.

I went inside and wondered what the future would bring.

Mercifully, the future brought promise. My daughter, who in another era might have been institutionalized, learned, over time, to read, write and do simple math in the presence of dedicated and talented teachers. She also sat in on history and science and physical education classes, performing to the best of her ability. Same age students without disabilities set an example for her. She grew to be curious and talkative and impish, and her general education peers loved her. The arrangement was good for everyone, good for the ways it broadened people's perspectives. She went to basketball games with her friends. She walked across the stage in a cap and gown at commencement. (I wept tears of joy when this happened.) She got a service job in a college cafeteria. Everyone knew she'd never discover the cure for cancer or design a house or fly a plane, but it didn't matter. She was making contributions to the world. She was teaching others how to be compassionate and open minded. Pointing out the wonder of simple things. Proving that when given a chance, anyone can rise to the occasion.

Sometimes I think about my own childhood: my mother, and the lessons she taught me. I grew up in an idyllic community, a happy child, a lucky child. Mine was, at the time, a community of white, post-war, middle class Americans looking forward to the promise of suburban ideals. I only learned about disabled people by happenstance: every now and then, I stumbled across one. They weren't hidden, exactly. But they weren't a part of my life, either. They were like unfortunate secrets that tumbled out at inopportune times.

Once I saw a man with legs cut off at the knees, perhaps a veteran, who sat on a wooden pallet and begged for handouts in front of the department store. I was four or five years old and coming to grips with the fact that the world was bigger than myself. It was a cold, grey day and he was bundled up in a jacket, his hands holding a can out in front of him. When I walked past him, I pulled in close to my mother and turned my face, afraid of the ways he was different from everyone I knew.

And then there was a woman, perhaps in her early thirties, who rode an inflated inner tube on the lake I loved to swim in. She had dark brown hair and a wide open face. She was euphoric splashing around with the little kids who frolicked near the shore. Ten or twelve years old at the time, I was embarrassed for her. Embarrassed that she didn't realize how out of place she was, that she was acting like a four-year-old in that bulbous body ... that she was so strange. I cast my eyes away and kept walking until the sounds of splashing and children's squeals were behind me.

There was, most memorably, a boy who rode the bus to school with me and a brood of other junior high students in the early

1960s. He was the one who made me ache inside. His was the last bus stop and he was always alone. Every day the bus driver pulled up alongside him, no matter the weather – and it was often freezing cold with sleet or snow – and there he'd be, skinny and bespectacled, his brown hair parted on the left and combed neatly back, standing with a briefcase full of school supplies in his left hand. The bus driver slid the lever to the side and the folding door whooshed open to let him board.

As he climbed on the bus, he shifted that briefcase over and clamped it tightly under his all but useless right arm, so he could use his left hand to hold on to the rail and help himself up the steps. It looked painful. And hard. He couldn't extend his right arm, or his contracted, claw-like hand, which he held close to his chest, the way a soldier holds his hat at his heart.

It seemed to me like his right side was rebelling. He limped on his right leg, and so, briefcase clamped, right leg limping, he made his way awkwardly onto the bus, where he stood silently in the aisle, just behind the driver, staring ahead with expressionless eyes for the duration of the fifteen-minute ride to school. He stood because no other kid on that bus was going to make room for him. It was like everyone thought he was contagious, like everyone thought if they acknowledged him they'd be next on the shunned list. He was too uncomfortable to ask for a seat. Too aware of his own differences.

I knew better. My mother had taught me better. My conscience told me that what was happening wasn't right, or necessary. I remember sitting about four rows back by the window, hunkering down, feeling sorry for him and trying to summon the courage to say, "You can sit by me." When I finally did, he sat down without speaking, clamped his briefcase, turned his shoulders and knees toward the aisle, and the two of us rode to the school in silence, being careful not to touch one another.

Sometimes I talked to my mother about these people, my confusion and my fears, usually in the kitchen when she was cooking or washing dishes. It was a warm and safe environment where I could open up. She listened then said, "There but for the grace of God go you," turning to look into my face. Her truth had a penetrating effect.

I knew what she meant: It was fortune that placed me where I was, how I was, when I was. I had a good life, a prosperous life. I should be grateful.

I remember reading, when I was a teenager, about a mother whose child was born disabled in the 1940s or 50s. I don't recall her name or her child's, or even the title of her story, but it left an imprint on me, one that I couldn't help but personalize after my daughter was born.

What I recollect is one of those arresting scenes. The mother standing in a window watching her adolescent daughter crawl across the front yard because she couldn't walk. The mother had been advised to institutionalize her child, but had refused. Instead, she raised and loved her daughter and set her free in the only way that was available to her. She let her go outside to play, come what may.

I recognize that my daughter's life and my own are as fulfilling as they are because of the courage of parents like this woman – people who took up the yoke, braved the status quo, and fought for the rights of their disabled children. They were visionaries, and I am thankful for them. I am thankful that my daughter was born into this enlightened era.

At least, I thought it was an enlightened era.

As I write this, many in the country find themselves shaken and disoriented by the election of Donald Trump to the United States presidency, me among them. One reason is that just when America seemed to have truly accepted the rights and dignity of the disabled, and to have provided a range of opportunity, Trump went on a platform and mocked disabled New York Times reporter, Serge Kovaleski.

Trump held his right hand up by his shoulder and flapped it around uselessly, as if it were nothing more than a fish on a line. He affected a manic voice and whined.

Kovaleski very much reminds me of the boy I invited to sit next to me on the bus – combed hair, glasses, right arm, hand, and all. I am deeply offended by Trump's insensitivity. This grown man, this privileged man, this would be world leader, acting as bad as, if not worse, than those junior high kids on the bus.

In another stunning turn, this time as President, he nominated billionaire Betsy DeVos, a devotee of private and charter schools, to be his Secretary of Education. On February 7, 2017 she was confirmed, and part of her job will be enforcing the federal IDEA law, which she admitted during her Senate hearing that she 'might be confused' about.

Their ignorance and apparent lack of caring knock the wind out of me. It is extraordinarily painful to think that these two who have our children's future in their hands, have no greater respect for the most vulnerable among us than this.

What is obvious is that their lives haven't been touched personally by disabled children. Had one of their sons or daughters been born with cerebral palsy or developmental disability or blindness or deafness or autism, or any of the other handicapping conditions that can strike a person, this whole conversation would not be happening.

As the old adage reminds us, "Experience is a great teacher."

This is why a public education for the disabled, in the least restrictive environment, is so important. The IDEA law broadens and enhances everyone's life. Exposure, companionship, sharing – these experiences make us better people. An enlightened, just and compassionate people.

SCAMP, the aforementioned camp for disabled children, meets every summer to bridge the months when the schools are on vacation. The goal, in addition to its social outlet, is to help its disabled students maintain and use what they've learned. It attracts hundreds of disabled children from across the county.

In many ways it is a partner to our school system, since it is staffed by able-bodied teachers, paraprofessionals, therapists, aids, and, importantly, many teens who volunteer. Because of SCAMP, and the interactions that take place between the disabled and their 'normal' peers in the public schools, a healthy camaraderie has become second nature. Because of the visibility of the disabled in our community, we are not a community of prejudice or ignorance, but of prosperity.

People like Trump and DeVos could learn a great deal from us.

We cannot afford as a populace to be represented by people who mock the disabled and are confused about their rights. Too much is at stake – for everyone.

My mother has been dead for four years now. Before she died she watched me raise Jennifer using the lessons she taught me, and she watched my daughter thrive through her public education and subsequent employment. I like to think Mom's ghost is standing just at my shoulder, listening, commiserating. We speak sometimes, wishing our words could reach Donald Trump and Betsy DeVos: "There but for the grace of Goåd go you."

"ALL YOU NEED IS LOVE …" JOHN LENNON

STEVE NELSON

Steve Nelson, Head of Calhoun School 1998-2017 in NYC, one of America's most notable progressive schools, and Author of "First Do No Harm: Progressive Education in a Time of Existential Risk" (Garn Press)

"All you need is love …" – John Lennon

Friday, January 20th, Donald J. Trump was inaugurated as the 45th President of these not-so-United States.

Saturday, January 21st, millions of humans of all identities gathered around the globe to march, sing and love one another. It was the golden sun after the rain, the rediscovery of the deep blue firmament after clouds lifted.

I choose Saturday.

Of course we can't just love each other and ignore Friday. "America First!" proclaimed the President. His cabinet appointments and executive orders threaten decades of social progress. The new President's first petty act was to remove a $500 FHA mortgage benefit for working class folks. LGBTQ rights and climate change vanished from the White House website on day one. His first speech as President was about himself, his victory, and lies about the size of his adoring crowd. (Lies about size are his trademark.)

So we will resist, we will protest, we will march and we will fight. But most of all, we must love.

I felt great despair on election night. But I don't despair now. I've come to see this dark moment in American history as the death rattle of intolerance and injustice. It is the final ugly expression of resentment over social progress – civil rights, gay rights, women's rights. It is the angry sigh of Americans who feel left behind and blame those who are further behind. It is the subconscious longing to preserve the assumed privilege that has been mistaken for the natural order. It is the imbalance felt by millions of white men as the world levels off and "the others" walk confidently among them.

History suggests that children tend to lean toward their parents' political values. But history need not repeat itself. Students at a public school in Illinois sponsored a "Walk a Mile in Her Hijab" event. When gay students were attacked in Texas, their classmates protested in the streets. The great cultural divide between the adult coastal "elites" and "flyover country" Trumpians doesn't exist among the vast majority of young folks. They are, by and large, accepting and generous of spirit.

And, as we all know, we are only a few decades away from being a majority minority nation. Even a wall along the border can't change this inevitability. Only stopping reproduction could slow the coming of that day – and white evangelical conservatives are committed to limiting access to birth control! The irony is sublime.

During the presidential campaign, the Clinton folks borrowed from the elegant and powerful Michelle Obama. "When they go low, we go high." This is not the same as the Christian imperative to turn the other cheek. Going high does not mean going silently. It means speaking truth to power with dignity. It is putting a flower in a rifle barrel. It means not fighting fire with fire, but extinguishing fire by not giving it the oxygen of our attention.

And the very "highest" we can go is to love our children. The children in our homes, the children in other's homes, the children in the streets and most of all, the children in our schools.

This includes the child in Donald Trump's home. On the Sunday after inauguration, Facebook reported nasty remarks about 10 year-old Barron Trump. Shameful. He was the only light that pierced the inaugural gloom as he played peekaboo with his nephew while his father signed executive orders. His small face was fully alive in contrast to the grim pomp and "America First!" exhortations from his father. I wonder if Donald ever played peekaboo with Barron? I wonder if Fred Trump ever played peekaboo with little Donald?

I wonder because I know Donald Trump was not born evil. He too was once a small boy, ready to absorb whatever filled his life, whether unconditional love or unbearable pain. In one way or another, we all fulfill the prophetic acts that are visited on or withheld from us. If love is conditional or absent, callouses grow on the inside and eventually encase the heart because it cannot bear further assault. A narcissist has an insatiable appetite for adoration – not because it feels good, but because it can't be felt no matter how persistently sought. If love for a child is unconditional and generous, narcissism is impossible, because the heart is open and feels deeply. We can't be sure what acts were visited on or withheld from our President during his childhood, but a 2016

New York Times article hints at the family dynamic:

> *Mr. Trump (Donald) said that their father (Fred) "could be unyielding," and that (brother) Freddy had struggled with his abundant criticism and stinginess with praise.*
>
> *"For me, it worked very well," Mr. Trump said. "For Fred (Jr.), it wasn't something that was going to work."*

It is a familiar pattern. A child of an abundantly critical parent who is stingy with praise might crumble and self-medicate as did Freddy Trump, an alcoholic who died at age 43. Or such a child might grow callouses of narcissism and become a desperately tweeting President of the United States. It didn't work very well for either of them.

What they both needed was love.

For millions of children, school is the most dependable place they might get the love they need. The fight for justice has many fronts: Health rights, labor rights, reproductive rights, economic rights, gender rights and more. We must reverse climate change before it reverses human existence. It can seem overwhelming. But it must start with education. If we engage on all the other fronts but don't preserve education rights, we will fail. If we preserve education and lead our children toward love, democracy and empathy, all the other matters will eventually yield to a mighty wave of justice.

In my recent book, *First Do No Harm: Progressive Education in a Time of Existential Risk*, I offer an Educational Bill of Rights wherein I write that all parents should expect schools to:

> *Recognize the broad consensus that early childhood education should be primarily dedicated to free, imaginative play*
>
> *Provide arts programming, recognizing that the arts are*

critical to all learning and to understanding the human experience

Provide ample physical movement, both in physical education classes and in other ways, recognizing that exercise enhances learning for all children

Exhibit, in structure and practice, awareness that children develop at different rates and in different ways; that strict age- or grade-level standards and expectations are meaningless and damaging

Acknowledge the large body of evidence that long hours of homework are unnecessary and detract from children's (and families') quality of life

Exhibit genuine *affection and respect for all children*

Honor a wide range of personalities and temperaments

Encourage curiosity, risk-taking and creativity

Cultivate and sustain intrinsic motivation rather than relying on elaborate extrinsic systems of rewards and punishment

Understand that brain research supports active learning, engaging all the senses

Understand that children are intelligent in multiple ways and that all these intelligences should be honored and developed

Listen to all children's voices, give them real experience in democratic processes, and allow them to express their individuality

Know each child well, appreciate the unique mix of quali-

ties each child brings, and never demean, discourage or humiliate any child

The current education reform movement violates nearly every one of these educational rights. Too many of America's schools are sterile or punitive. Children are being humiliated and discouraged. In his inauguration speech, Trump claimed that schools are flush with cash and depriving children of "all knowledge." It is far more accurate to note that schools are deprived of both cash and love.

We can resist, protest, march and fight. But our most urgent need is to demand an educational system that provides an equitable, accessible, humane and engaging public school for every child in America. We need a school system that brings America's children together, not one that divides them through the propaganda of "choice."

We need schools that love children unconditionally and invite our children to love each other. And we need schools that encourage our children to love the world so much that they will save it.

A MINORITY PRESIDENT: WHY THE POLLS FAILED, AND WHAT THE MAJORITY CAN DO

GEORGE LAKOFF

George Lakoff, Professor Emeritus of Cognitive Science and Linguistics, is a World Renowned Linguist Integrating Studies of Social Issues and Politics from a Neural Linguistics Perspective

The American Majority

Hillary Clinton won the majority of votes in this year's presidential election.

The loser, for the majority of voters, will now be a minority president-elect. Don't let anyone forget it. Keep referring to Trump as the minority president, Mr. Minority and the overall Loser. Constant repetition, with discussion in the media and over social media, questions the legitimacy of the minority president to ignore the values of the majority. The majority, at the very least, needs to keep its values in the public eye and view the minority president's action through majority American values.

The polls failed and the nation needs to know why. The pollsters and pundits have not given a satisfactory answer.

I will argue that the nature of mind is not a mere technical issue for the cognitive and brain sciences, but that it had everything to do with the outcome of the 2016 election – and the failure of the pollsters, the media, and Democrats to predict it. They were not alone. The public needs to understand better how the human mind works in general – but especially in politics. There is a lot to know. Let us go step by step.

The Mind

I am a cognitive scientist. I study the human mind. Our minds are neural minds. The mind is physical, constituted by the neural circuitry of our brains and bodies. Most thought is unconscious, since we don't have conscious access to our neural circuitry. Conscious thought is a small part of thought – estimates by neuroscientists vary between a general "most" to as much as 98%, with consciousness as the tip of the mental iceberg. We do know that people tend to make decisions unconsciously before becoming consciously aware of them. How the neural unconscious functions in decision-making is vitally important for politics.

Worldviews and Worldview Differences

Our fixed worldviews are made up of complex ideas carried out by relatively fixed neural circuitry. Our worldviews determine how we think the world operates, as well as how we think it should operate. In short, our worldviews are constituted by neural circuitry for what we understand as normal, and what we take as right and wrong.

There are, of course, radical differences in worldview, and we see those differences in politics, religion, culture, and so on.

Here is the crucial fact about worldview differences: We can only understand what our brain circuitry allows us to understand. If facts don't fit the worldviews in our brains, the facts may not even be noticed – or they may be puzzling, or ignored, or rejected outright, or if threatening, attacked. All of these happen in politics. A global warming denier does not say, "I am denying science." The facts just don't fit his worldview and don't make sense to him or her.

Consider some all too real examples.

- If you have an evangelical religious belief that the End Days are near, when the believers will be swept up to Heaven and the evil people left behind destroyed. The issue will be whether you will be saved, not the planet.

- Suppose you believe, as many do, that laissez-faire capital-ism is both natural and supremely moral. The most impor-tant, natural, and right thing to do would be to maximize your profits, and those of the firms you invest in, while you are alive on earth. Then it will make sense to maximize fossil fuel profits. Passing them up for the sake of the planet will not make sense.

- Suppose you are a small-time rancher with a small herd of cattle in a remote area of a red state, living next to a federal nature preserve where there are endangered species. You work hard, have a hard time making a living, cannot afford expensive feed for you cattle, and think you should be able to have your cattle graze on the "unused" publicly-owned land next door so you can make ends meet. So you just tear down the fence and drive your cattle in. The feds tell you to leave, but the Republican governor tells the state police to leave you alone, and the Republican elected judge rules for you over the government. You feel morally vindicated.

You can only make sense of what the neural circuitry characterizing your worldview allows you to make sense of.

What about undeniable all-important facts that violate one's moral worldview, like the Trump election? That can result in shock, physical shock. We will discuss why below.

What is a Political Moderate?

- A moderate has a major worldview and an opposite minor worldview.

- A moderate conservative has mostly conservative views, but some progressive views.

- A moderate progressive has mostly progressive views, but some conservative views.

- There is no political ideology shared by all moderates.

- There is no consistent political "middle."

Bi-conceptuals

In order to be a moderate, you have to hold two opposing worldviews at once, but apply them to different issues. How can you have two opposing worldviews in the same brain, when each is a fixed neural circuit? Easy. They "inhibit" each other: turning one on turns the other off. This is called mutual inhibition. It is common in the brain.

Political change has worked through bi-conceptualism –

through moving minor worldviews in a more major direction, by "strengthening" minor worldviews until they become major.

Frames

A worldview is an overall conceptual framework you use to understand the world. It is made up of mental "frames," which are used to understand situations. A restaurant frame contains waiters/ waitresses), customers, tables and chairs, a chef, a menu, food, a check, and so on, together with expectations about what each will do. Political worldviews are complexes of political frames that fit together coherently.

Words have meanings that are defined relative to conceptual frames. If you hear "Here's the dinner menu", you know you're in a restaurant. If you hear, "What's the easiest way to eliminate the Department of Education?", you know you're with the Trump transition team.

Language in Politics

In politics, institutions, and cultural life, words tend not to be neutral. Instead their meanings are defined with respect to political worldviews. There are conservative and liberal vocabularies. "Save the planet!" is liberal. "Energy independence" is a conservative 'dog whistle.' It means dig coal and drill for oil and gas, even on public lands, and don't invest seriously in solar and wind. Some might think those are politically neutral expressions. If you take them literally and ignore worldview differences, you might think everyone should want to save the planet and everyone should want energy independence. Liberals want literal energy independence, but through sustainable energy like solar and wind. Conservatives don't believe in man-made climate change and want energy independence through maximizing coal, gas, and oil. Politically charged meanings put the other side in a bind. The opposition cannot answer directly. You won't hear conservatives say "I don't want to save the planet," nor liberals say, "I'm against energy independence." Instead they have to change the frame.

In general, negating a frame just activates the frame and makes it stronger. I wrote a book called "Don't Think of an Elephant!" to make that point. Liberals are often caught in this trap. If a conservative says, "we should have tax relief," she is using the metaphor that taxation is an affliction that we need relief from. If a liberal replies, "No, we don't need tax relief," she is accepting the idea that taxation is an affliction. The first thing that is, or should be, taught about political language is not to repeat the language of the other side or negate their framing of the issue.

The Clinton campaign consistently violated the lesson of Don't Think of an Elephant! They used negative campaigning, assuming they could turn Trump's most outrageous words against him. They kept running ads showing Trump forcefully expressing views that liberals found outrageous. Trump supporters liked him for forcefully saying things that liberals found outrageous. They were ads paid for by the Clinton campaign that raised Trump's profile with his potential supporters!

The basic lesson comes from a legendary story in framing circles. Lesley Stahl interviewed Ronald Reagan, bringing up stinging criticisms of Reagan. The morning after the interview ran on TV Reagan's chief of staff called Stahl and thanked her for the interview. "But I was criticizing him," Stahl replied. The response was jovial, "But if you turned off the sound, he looked terrific. The presidential image is what will be remembered."

The more neural circuits are activated, the more the stronger their synapses get, and so the more easily they can be activated again and the more likely they will become permanent. The more the public hears one side's language, or sees one side's images, the more that side's frames will be activated, and the more that side's worldview will be strengthened in the brains of those who watch and listen. This is why political communication systems matter.

Think for a moment of the conservative Leadership Institute's 20th anniversary boast that they had trained over 159,000 local conservatives spokespeople from all over America in 20 years. Think of 159,000 trained conservative local leaders and spokes-people spread over all those red states on the 2016 presidential electoral map, in addition to Fox News and Rush Limbaugh. That is how working white men and women, who might have started out as liberals or moderates years ago, gradually became more conservative by hearing conservative language day after day.

And it was through such repetitive exposure every day to Trump's forceful language and forceful image, through free media and social media, that a great many people were affected.

Metaphors We Vote By

Much of unconscious thought is metaphorical. Not fanci-ful or "poetic" metaphors, but everyday ones we generally don't notice. We understand More as being Up, as in "Turn up the radio," which does not mean to throw it up to the ceiling. We understand achieving goals as reaching destinations: "You'll get there. There's nothing standing in your way. We can see the light at the end of the tunnel." The many metaphorical expressions reveal the presence of a conceptual metaphor, a mode of metaphorical thought. There's nothing special about metaphorical thought. Given commonplace experience in the world and given a neural system, thousands of everyday metaphorical thoughts arise spontaneously. It happens around the world, and it mostly goes unnoticed, carried out by your neural system.

Certain kinds of metaphorical thought, which go largely unnoticed, are central to our politics, as we shall see.

Values Over Demographics

Briefly, the polls failed because they work by demography, using census data, and other readily accessible data. The census tells us where people live, their age, gender, ethnicity, educational level, marital status, income level, etc. These are objective data, and this kind of data is easy to get and sample. But demographic data leaves out what is most important in elections and in political polling generally: Values! One's sense of right and wrong. That omission was crucial in this election.

It is not just crucial in polling. It is also crucial in journalism. Most people in the press also talk as if demography were the gold standard of political truth: the suburban educated women, the Hispanics, the white working class – all defined by demographics. But the relationship between voting and demographics is not one-to-one. This election showed that in spades. Many progressives think the same way: Demography and issues – issue by issue. Democrats looking for donors will ask, "What is your most important issue?" Instead, the values that define one's deepest identity are what matters most. Polling issue-by-issue misses the overall values that are all too often primary in elections.

Indeed, the very question, "What is your most important issue?" almost guarantees that climate change will barely enter the electoral debate. What comes to mind when the question is asked are relatively immediate concerns – jobs, health care, immigration, poverty, student debt, and so on. Global warming is not seen as imminent – it comes in about number 20 on the list of voters' "most important issues."

Part of the reason is that the causal link between global warming and weather disasters is not direct, but is a result of systemic factors in the ecosystem. High temperatures over the Pacific produce more evaporation, which means high energy water molecules go into the air, blow northeast and in winter come down as snow in Washington – more than ever before! The weather disasters throughout the country – severe hurricanes, floods, droughts, fires, – are often systemically caused by global warming and they should be named as such – a global warming hurricane, a climate change flood, a global warming drought, global warming fires – with illustrations of the systemic steps involved in the cause. To establish a frame, you need a name.

I've been studying such matters from the perspective of the neural mind for two decades, starting with Moral Politics (now in its Third Edition) and in seven books and dozens of papers, as well as with those doing survey and experimental research. Because this perspective has not been part of the public discourse, it is worth going over in some detail.

All Politics Is Moral

When a political leader proposes a policy, the assumption it that the policy is right, not wrong or morally irrelevant.

No political leader says, "Do what I say because it's evil. It's the devil's work, but do it!" Nor will a political leader say, "My policy proposal is morally irrelevant. It's neither right nor wrong. It doesn't really matter. Just do it."

When political leaders have opposing policies, that means they have opposing moral worldviews.

Why do voters vote their values?

Everyone likes to think of himself or herself as a good person.

That means that your moral system is a major part of your identity – who you most deeply are. Voting against your moral identity would be a rejection of self.

That is why poor conservatives vote against their material interests. They are voting for their moral worldviews to dominate, and for public respect for their values.

The Mystery

In the 1990's, as part of my research in the cognitive and brain sciences, I undertook to answer a question in my field: How do the various policy positions of conservatives and progressives hang together? Take conservatism: What does being against abortion have to do with being for owning guns? What does owning guns have to do with denying the reality of global warming? How does being anti-government fit with wanting a stronger military? How can you be pro-life and for the death penalty? How do these conservative positions make sense together? Progressives have the opposite views. How do their views hang together?

The Nation as Family Metaphor

The answer came from a realization that we tend to understand the nation metaphorically in family terms: We have founding fathers. We send our sons and daughters to war. We have homeland security. The conservative and progressive worldviews dividing our country can most readily be understood in terms of moral worldviews that are encapsulated in two very different idealizations of family life: The Nurturant Parent family (progressive) and the Strict Father family (conservative).

Why Idealizations of the Family?

What do social issues and their politics have to do with idealizations of the family? We are first governed in our families, and so we grow up understanding governing institutions in terms of the governing systems of families. Those governing institutions can be classrooms, teams, armies, churches, businesses, and so on. Nurturant and Strict family models pervade our culture.

Idealized Nurturant Families

Nurturance starts with empathy. In nurturant families, caring for a child requires knowing what the child needs and wants. It requires open, two-way conversation. Parents have to take care of themselves if they are to care of their children. For their well-being, children need clear limits and guidelines (Don't put your hand on a hot stove. You'll get burned.), personal responsibilities ("Brush your teeth"), and family responsibilities ("Take care of your sister. Set the table.") Children also need to empathize with others and act on that empathy. If not, as Barack Obama said his 2008 Father's Day speech, we'll have a generation of people who don't care about anybody else. Children also need to be fulfilled in life, and for this they need education, exercise, good health, a connection to nature, and a warm social life. And if some children require special attention, either because they are very young, or ill, or injured, or have other inherent problems, the rest of the family has to step up to help out.

Nurturance and Progressive Values

These family values map via metaphor onto progressive political values: Citizens care about other citizens and act through their government to provide public resources for all, for both businesses and individuals. That's how America started. The genius of the founding fathers centered on public resources. The public resources used by businesses were not only roads and bridges, but public education, a national bank, a patent office, courts for business cases, interstate commerce support, and of course the criminal justice system. From the beginning, the private depended on public resources – both private enterprise and private life. In private life, there were laws to protect freedoms and basic rights, as well as resources like police protection, public education, a national currency, access to banks for loans, courts for redress of grievances, and goods made available through interstate commerce.

Over time public resources have grown to include sewers, water and electricity, government protections in the form of "regulations" to keep unscrupulous corporations from harming the public, and to keep banks, mortgage holders, and investment houses from cheating the public. As commerce grew, the need for protective regulations grew into whole regulatory agencies of government. Modern life now depends on even more public resources, such as research universities and research support: computer science (via the NSF), the internet (from ARPA), pharmaceuticals and modern medicine (via the NIH), satellite communication (NASA and NOAA), and GPS systems and cell phones (satellite systems maintained with security and unbelievable precision by the Defense Department).

Private enterprise and private life utterly depend on public resources. Not on "the government." But on "the public." What these public resources provide is freedom: freedom to start and run a business, and freedom in private life. You're not free if you are not educated; your possibilities in life are limited. You're not free, if you have cancer and no health insurance. You're not free if you have no income – or not enough for basic needs. And if you work for a large company, you may not be free without a union. Unions free workers from corporate servitude – free working people to have a living wage, safety on the job, regular working hours, a pension, health benefits, dignity.

All of this arises from basic progressive values – empathy and care for one another – at the level of the nation.

The Strict Father and Conservative Values

In the strict father family, father knows best. He knows right from wrong and has the ultimate authority to make sure his children and his spouse do what he says, which is taken to be what is right. Many conservative spouses accept this worldview, uphold the father's authority, and are strict in those realms of family life that they are in charge of.

When his children disobey, it is the strict father's moral duty to punish them painfully enough so that, to avoid punishment, they will obey him (do what is right) and not just do what feels good. Through physical discipline they are supposed to become disciplined, internally strong, and able to prosper in the external world. What if they don't prosper? That means they are not disciplined, and therefore cannot be moral, and so deserve their poverty.

This reasoning shows up in conservative politics in which the poor are seen as lazy and undeserving, and the rich as deserving their wealth. Responsibility is thus taken to be personal responsibility not social responsibility. What you become is only up to you; society has nothing to do with it. You are responsible for yourself, not for others, who are responsible for themselves.

The Moral Hierarchy

The strict father logic extends further. The basic idea is that authority is justified by morality (the strict father version), and that, in a world ordered by nature, there should be (and traditionally has been) a moral hierarchy in which those who have traditionally dominated should dominate.

The hierarchy is: God above Man, Man above Nature, The Disciplined (Strong) above the Undisciplined (Weak), The Rich above the Poor, Employers above Employees, Adults above Children, Western culture above other cultures, America above other countries. The hierarchy extends to: Men above women, Whites above Nonwhites, Christians above non-Christians, Straights above Gays.

On the whole, conservative policies flow from the strict father worldview and this hierarchy. Trump is an extreme case, though very much in line with conservative policies.

Strict Father Complexities

There are political policies that follow from strict father morality. As we discuss them, please bear in mind that many if not most conservatives are bi-conceptual, that is, that have a strict father major worldview and a nurturant minor worldview on some issues or other.

In-Group Nurturance: More importantly, it is common for conservatives to show in-group nurturance – care for members of some in-group. What counts as an in-group varies.

- The minimal in-group is your family.

- The in-group can be members of your church or your religion – and the church or religion may offer help to the needy members of the church or religion.

- The in-group can be in the military, with military family getting housing, education, health care, and cheaper goods on the military base, and where platoon-members ("bands of brothers") are taken care of and never left behind.

- In small towns all over America where people are mostly conservative, the in-group can be community members and whoever lives in the town. The small-town nurturance for long-term neighbors can override differences in politics, race, ethnicity, gender, sexuality, and so on.

This means that in national or state politics, one may be a typical conservative, but those political views can be adjusted locally by moderation or in-group nurturance. Part of the conservative revolution of 1994 was the move by Newt Gingrich to rid the Republican party of moderates by running extreme conservatives against them in primaries.

It is also important to remember that moderate progressives are biconceptuals, that they have a minor conservative worldview on a certain issues, and that they can be made more conservative by repeated conservative language

Strict Father Political Policies

The most obvious strict father political policies are the following, group by group.

White Evangelical Christians:

Right-wing white evangelicals offer you a strict father God you are to fear – who can send you to burn in hell for eternity. Sinners get a second chance, to become "born again." After that, sinners who don't follow his commandments will burn in hell. Those who follow the commandments will be "saved."

The moral hierarchy creates a white evangelical politics:

- God above Man: Churches get major tax breaks, and seek public funding for religious schools.

- Men Above Women: Men get to decide on reproduction. Against Planned Parenthood, abortion, and morning-after pills. For laws requiring spousal and parental notification prior to abortion.

- Marriage between a man and a woman: no gay marriage.

- Child-rearing should follow the strict father model.

- Religious Christmas scenes in public places funded by public money.

- Large crosses erected on public land.

- The Ten Commandments in courtrooms.

- Political candidates must proclaim their religion.

Laissez-Faire Free Marketeers:

Corporations and those who own and run them are metaphorical strict fathers. Corporations are "persons" who can engage in political lobbying, who seek to maximize their profits, set rules for their employees and can punish them in various ways, ultimately by firing them or laying them off.

Corporate conservatives want laissez-faire free markets, where wealthy people and corporations set market rules in their favor with minimal government regulation and enforcement. They see taxation not as investment in publicly provided resources for all citizens, but as government taking their earnings (their private property) and giving the money through government programs to those who don't deserve it. This is the source of establishment Republicans' anti-tax and shrinking government views. This version of conservatism is quite happy with outsourcing to increase profits by sending manufacturing and many services abroad where labor is cheap, with the consequence that well-paying jobs leave America and wages are driven down here. They profit from many cheap imports important for business profits, such as steel, building materials, electronic parts, etc.

They also want to privatize public resources as much as possible: eliminate public schools, publicly financed health insurance, drill and mine on public lands, build private highways, and so on.

The White Working Class:

Many members of the white working class have strict father morality, even those in unions. Many have their strict father views limited to their home life, but many have them as a major worldview. As conservatives, they believe in individual responsibility not government "handouts;" they may resent union dues and prefer "right to work" laws; and they may implicitly accept the moral hierarchy and believe they are superior to nonwhites, Latinos, non-Christians, and gays and should be in a higher financial and social position.

Conservative women may accept their position as inferior to their men, but still see themselves above the rest of the hierarchy. The white working class has been hit hard by income inequality, globalization and outsourcing, computerization, the decline of coal mining, low-wage chain stores driving out small business, and if older, ageism. They are largely uneducated and see themselves as looked down on by the educated "elite" who tell them that everyone should go to college to merit today's jobs.

They also resent "political correctness," which directs resources to those who need them even more, but are lower on the conservative moral hierarchy. They want the respect of being on the right side of politics, of having their moral views – and hence their deepest identity – confirmed.

Political Correctness

Nurturant parent morality puts a premium on helping those in the family who need it the most: infants, sick or injured children, and so on.

In liberal politics, those lower on the conservative moral hierarchy are seen to have been victimized by those who are more powerful. The result is a reverse moral hierarchy, in which the less powerful are more deserving of assistance than the more powerful: the poor more than the non-poor, non-white more than white, women more than men, immigrants more than residents, and so on.

The white working class calls this view "political correctness." It leaves out poor whites, especially in nonurban areas, who have had to face the problems of a culture that, as we have just seen, has been devastated by corporate greed (income inequality, globalization and outsourcing, computerization, and low-wage chain stores driving out small business) and factors like the decline of coal mining.

All three of these groups – evangelicals, corporatists, and the white working class correctly saw the Supreme Court issue as central to upholding their values across the board, on all issues.

The Main Issue Is Identity

For each type of conservative, the main issue is one's identity, which is defined by strict father values. One can have a religious version, a business version, or a working class resentment version, but in each case self-identity is the issue. That is why those who voted for Trump didn't care if he constantly lied, or if he treated women outrageously, or if he was ignorant of foreign policy. What mattered was the voter's moral identity, the voter's sense of right and wrong, the voter's self-respect as a conservative.

Trump and those in his campaign understood this. Those in the Democratic party, the media, and pollsters did not.

Why the Moral Indicators Were Missed

Corporatist Republican leaders tended to study business economics in college, and as a result studied marketing. Marketing professors study the mind and how people really think: using frames, metaphors, narratives, images, and emotions – mostly applied to advertising. These Republican leaders learned how to market their ideas.

Progressives who go to college with a primary concentration on politics tend to study political science, law, public policy, and economic theory. Those courses of study almost never include cognitive science, neuroscience, and cognitive linguistics – and so progressives interested in politics don't learn about the Neural Mind, that is, about unconscious thought, frames, conceptual metaphors, moral worldviews, the role of language, etc.

Instead, they are taught a version of Enlightenment reason, following René Descartes around 1650, namely:

- that all thought is conscious

- that reason is a matter of logic, as in a mathematical proof

- that since reason defines what means to be human, all rational people reason according to logic

- and therefore, if you give everybody the facts, they ought to all reason to the right conclusion.

This is an utterly false theory of reason – taught as rationality and "critical thinking." It was vitally important during the Enlightenment because it taught that people could think for themselves and did not have to follow the thinking the kings and religious leaders. One might like it to be true, but it isn't.

False Reason, False Analyses

The polls, the media, and the Democratic Party all failed to understand conservative values and their importance. They failed to understand unconscious thought and moral worldviews. While hailing science in the case of climate change, they ignored science when it came to their own minds. The pollsters, given easy access to demographics via census and other data, came up with their own view of mind, that demographics reflects public opinion, and that public opinion understood this way, drives elections. This amounts to a strange demographic theory of mind, that demography determines thought.

The demographic theory of mind is naturally paired with the view that people simply vote their material interests, that their interests vary, and hence that issues are separable. This is widely assumed, despite the well-known facts that poor conservatives and rich liberals of often vote against their material interests.

But it does make polling – and fund raising – easier. Just ask people what their most important issues are, or to what degree that are for or against a particular policy.

The Justifications

This type of polling has its justifications.

First, people with similar worldviews can tend to cluster in some demographic categories.

Second, most of polling is done by advertisers selling products. If the polls miss by differences as small as those between

Trump and Clinton, they are doing well by their clients.

Incidentally, polling methodology used in advertising leads to the view that candidates are products, to be sold like cars, pharmaceuticals, and beauty products, and have to establish a recognizable, popular brand.

It is true that moral worldviews generalize over specific issues, and so a specific issue can activate a general worldview. But the general moral worldview is not studied or discussed.

An Alternative

There is a way out that may be simple, but need to be tested. One can include questions about values, even if the values are unconscious. The technique was developed by Elisabeth Wehling, Matt Feinberg (U. of Toronto), Laura Saslow (U. of Michigan), and myself. It was based on the conceptual metaphor of the Nation As Family, with two types of families – strict and nurturant. Technically, a conceptual metaphor is a neural mapping, linking the frame structure of one domain (e.g., the values of a type of family) to another domain (e.g., political views about the nation).

Beginning with the theory proposed in my 1996 book, Moral Politics, we constructed two mappings linking family values to political values. We separated the family values from the political values and randomized each. We then asked, in surveys and experiments, the randomized questions to see if the correlations fit the predications of the mappings.

The correlations were overwhelming, and are reported in Elisabeth Wehling's 2013 doctoral dissertation, A nation under joint custody: How conflicting family models divide US-politics. The basic idea is that of a Moral Politics Scale that can be used in surveys, and that might be included in future polls. Questions about family values can be used as indicators of the moral values used in political worldviews. Other studies have been done and are in the publication pipeline.

A few early studies do not, and should not, create a field, but it is a beginning. Polling studies using these ideas need to be done.

Clever Trump

Democrats and most of the media looked upon Trump as a clown, a dimwit, a mere jerk, a reality show star, who did not understand the issues and who could not possibly win when he was insulting so many demographic groups. I am anything but a Trump fan, but I estimated that he would get about 47% of the vote. Although I was sure he wouldn't quite win, I kept warning people that he could, especially given the Democrats' failure to understand the role of values.

Nine months before the election I wrote about how Trump used the brains of people listening to him to his advantage. Here is a recap of how Trump does it, with examples taken from his campaign.

Unconscious thought works by certain basic mechanisms. Trump uses them instinctively to turn people's brains toward what he wants: Absolute authority, money, power, and celebrity.

The mechanisms are:

1. Words are neurally linked to the circuits that determine their meaning. The more a word is heard, the more the circuit is activated and the stronger it gets, and so the easier it is to fire again. Trump repeats. Win, Win. We're gonna win so much you'll get tired of winning.

2. Framing: Crooked Hillary. Framing Hillary as purposely

and knowingly committing crimes for her own benefit, which is what a crook does. Repeating makes many people unconsciously think of her that way, even though she has always been found to have been honest and legal by thorough studies by the right-wing Bengazi committee (which found nothing) and the FBI (which found nothing to charge her with.) Yet the framing worked.

There is a common metaphor that Immorality Is Illegality, and that acting against Strict Father Morality (the only kind of morality recognized) is being immoral. Since virtually everything Hillary Clinton has ever done has violated Strict Father Morality, that makes her immoral to strict conservatives. The metaphor makes her actions immoral, which makes her a crook. The chant "Lock her up!" activates this whole line of reasoning.

3. Well-known examples: When a well-publicized disaster happens, the coverage is repeated over and over, and watched on tv and read about many times. Neurally, the repetition activates the frame-circuitry for it over and over, strengthening the synapses with each repetition. Neural circuits with strong synapses can be activated more easily that those with weak synapses, and so the probability that they will be activated is higher. And so the frame is more likely to be activated.

Repeated examples of shootings by Muslims, African-Americans, and Latinos make it seem probable that it could happen to you. It thus raises fears that it could happen to you and your community – despite the miniscule actual probability. Trump uses this technique to create fear. Fear tends to activate desire for a strong strict father to protect you – namely, Trump.

4. Grammar: Radical Islamic terrorists: "Radical" puts Muslims on a linear scale and "terrorists" imposes a frame on

the scale, suggesting that terrorism is built into the religion itself. The grammar suggests that there is something about Islam that has terrorism inherent in it. Imagine calling the Charleston gunman a "radical Republican terrorist."

Trump is aware of this to at least some extent. As he said to Tony Schwartz, the ghost-writer who wrote The Art of the Deal for him, "I call it truthful hyperbole. It's an innocent form of exaggeration – and it's a very effective form of promotion."

5. Conventional metaphorical thought is inherent in our largely unconscious thought. Such normal modes of metaphorical thinking are not noticed as such. Consider Brexit, which used the metaphor of "entering" and "leaving" the EU.

There is a universal metaphor that states are bounded regions in space: you can enter a state, be deep in some state, and come out of that state. If you enter a café and then leave the café, you will be in the same location as before you entered.

But that need not be true of states of being. But that was the metaphor used with Brexit; Britons believed that after leaving the EU, things would be as before when the entered the EU. They were wrong. Things changed radically while they were in the EU.

That same metaphor is being used by Trump: Make America Great Again. Make America Safe Again. And so on. As if there was some past ideal state that we can go back to just by electing Trump.

6. There is also a metaphor that A Country Is a Person and a metonymy of the President Standing For the Country. Thus, Obama, via both metaphor and metonymy, can stand conceptually for America. Therefore, by saying that Obama is weak and not respected, it is communicated that America, with Obama as president, is weak and disrespected. The

inference is that it is because of Obama.

The corresponding inference is that, with a strong president like Trump, the country should be strong, and via strict father reasoning, respected.

7. The country as person metaphor and the metaphor that war or conflict between countries is a fistfight between people, leads to the inference that just having a strong president will guarantee that America will win conflicts and wars. Trump will just throw knockout punches. In his acceptance speech at the convention, Trump repeatedly said that he would accomplish things that, in reality, can only be done by the people acting with their government. After one such statement, there was a chant from the floor, "He will do it."

8. The metaphor that The nation Is a Family was used throughout the GOP convention. We heard that strong military sons are produced by strong military fathers and that "defense of country is a family affair." From Trump's love of family and commitment to their success, we are to conclude that, as president he will love America's citizens and be committed to the success of all.

9. There is a common metaphor that identifying with your family's national heritage makes you a member of that nationality. Suppose your grandparents came from Italy and you identify with your Italian ancestors, you may proudly state that you are Italian. The metaphor is natural. Literally, you have been American for two generations. Trump made use of this commonplace metaphor in attacking US District Court Judge Gonzalo Curiel, who is American, born and raised in the United States. Trump said he was a Mexican, and therefore would hate him and tend to rule against him in a case brought against Trump University for fraud.

10. Then there is the metaphor system used in the phrase "to call someone out." First the word "out." There is a general metaphor that Knowing Is Seeing as in "I see what you mean." Things that are hidden inside something cannot be seen and hence not known, while things are not hidden but out in public can be seen and hence known. To "out" someone is to make their private knowledge public. To "call someone out" is to publicly name someone's hidden misdeeds, thus allowing for public knowledge and appropriate consequences.

This is the basis for the Trumpian metaphor that Naming is Identifying. Thus naming your enemies will allow you to identify correctly who they are, get to them, and so allow you to defeat them. Hence, just saying "radical Islamic terrorists" allows you to pick them out, get at them, and annihilate them. And conversely, if you don't say it, you won't be able to pick them out and annihilate them. Thus a failure to use those words means that you are protecting those enemies – in this case Muslims, that is, potential terrorists because of their religion.

I could go on, but I think you get the idea. Our neural minds think in certain patterns. Trump knows how to exploit them. Whatever other limitations on his knowledge, he knows a lot about using your brain against you to acquire and maintain power and money.

The Media

It is vitally important for the public to be aware of how their brains can be used against them. Can the media do such a job? There are many forces militating against it.

First, there is obvious pressure on those reporting on politics in the media to assume that thought is conscious and not to talk about matters outside of public political discourse, that is, don't talk about things your audience can't understand.

Second, many in the media accept Enlightenment Reason. It is common for progressive pundits to quote conservative claims in conservative language and then argue against it, assuming that negating a frame will wipe it out, when instead negating a frame activates and strengthens the frame. They are ignoring the warnings of Don't Think of an Elephant!

Third, there is the metaphor that Objectivity is Balance, that interviews are about opinions and that opinions should be balanced.

Fourth, there are political and economic levers of power that are being used on the media. Trump is choosing the new members of the Federal Communications Commission, which has the power to take away broadcast licenses. The Congress has the power of the purse over National Public Broadcasting and one can already see where NPR correspondents are hesitant to challenge lies. Similarly, corporate advertisers have that power over radio and tv stations, as do their corporate owners.

Fifth, there are ratings, which mean advertising money. The head of CBS, Leslie Moonves, for example, said that CBS benefitted by giving Trump free airtime during the campaign. "It may not be good for America, but it's good for CBS," he said.

Sixth, it is virtually impossible during an interview to do instant fact-checking and constantly interrupting the interviewee to confront his lies, or at least report them. It would of course lead the interviewee to refuse future interviews with that reporter or that station – or keep him or her out of the White House Press Corps.

The result is media intimidation and steps toward the loss of the free press. The question is whether people in the media can join together in courage when their careers, and hence their livelihood, are threatened.

One possibility is for journalists to used more accurate language. Take government regulations. Their job is to protect the public from harm and fraud composed by unscrupulous corporations. The Trump administration wants to get rid of "regulations." They are actually getting rid of protection. Can journalists actually say they are get rid of protections, saying the word "protection," and reporting on the harm that would be done by not protecting the public.

Can the media report on corporate poisoning of the public – through introducing lead and other cancer-causing agents into the water through fracking and various manufacturing processes, through making food or toiletries that contain poisonous and cancer-causing ingredients, and on and on. The regulations are there for a purpose – protection. Can the media use the words POISON and CANCER? The public needs to know.

Seventh, there are science-of-mind constraints. Reporters and commentators are expected to stick to what is conscious and with literal meaning. But most real political discourse makes use of unconscious thought, which shapes conscious thought via unconscious framing and commonplace conceptual metaphors, as we have seen. Can the media figure out a way to say what is in this article?

More than ever we need courage and imagination in the media. It is crucial, for the history of the country and the world, as well as the planet.

What the Majority Can Do

A strong American Majority movement is necessary, and its backbone has to be a citizens' communication system – or systems – run through the internet, framing American values accurately and systemically day after day, telling truths framed by American majority moral values – and appealing honestly and forthrightly to those in-group nurturant values in small towns across America. The idea that must be brought across is empathy for those in your in-group, your town. This is basic progressive thought: citizens care about citizens and provide public resources for all, maximizing freedom. It fits in-group nurturance. And it undermines – rather than negates – strict father morality.

What a Strict Father Cannot Be

There are certain things that strict fathers cannot be: A Loser, Corrupt, and especially not a Betrayer of Trust.

Trump lost the popular vote. To the American majority, he is a Loser, a minority president. It needs to be said and repeated.

Above all, Trump is a Betrayer of Trust. He is acting like a dictator, and is even supporting Putin's anti-American policies.

He is betraying trust is a direct way, by refusing to put his business interests in a blind trust. By doing so, and by insisting on his children both running the business and getting classified information, he is using the presidency to make himself incredibly wealthy – just as Putin has. This is Corruption of the highest and most blatant level. Can the media say the words: Corruption, Betrayal of Trust? He ran on a promise to end corruption, to "drain the swamp" in Washington. Instead, he has brought a new and much bigger swamp with him – lobbyists put in charge of one government agency after another, using public funds and the power of the government to serve corporate greed. And the biggest crock in the swamp is Trump himself!

The Trump administration will wreak havoc on the very people who voted for him in those small towns – disaster after disaster. It will be a huge betrayal. The $500 billion in infrastructure – roads and bridges, airports, sewers, eliminating lead water pipes – will probably not make it to those thousands of small rural towns with in-group nurturance for the townspeople. How many factories with good-paying jobs can be brought to such towns? Not thousands. Many of those who voted for Trump will inevitably be among the 20 million who will lose their health care. And they will become even further victims of corporate greed – more profits going to the top one percent and more national corporations, say, fast food and big-box stores paying low wages and offering demeaning jobs will continue to wipe out local businesses. Will this be reported? Will it even be said? And if so, how will it be said in a way that doesn't wind up promoting Trump?

The American majority must create an online citizen communication network – or multiple networks – to spread its positive American values and truths as antidotes to those small towns with in-group nurturance as the Trump swamp swamps them!

The message is not merely negative, they are being betrayed. That's the Don't Think of an Elephant! trap. Rather it is that the town's in-group nurturance is nurturance. It works because care is morally right.

Right now the majority is fighting back, pointing out what is wrong with Trump day after day. In many cases, they are missing the message of Don't Think of an Elephant! By fighting against Trump, many protesters are just showcasing Trump, keeping him in the limelight, rather than highlighting the majority's positive moral view and viewing the problem with Trump from within the majority's positive worldview frame. To effectively fight for what is right, you have to first say what is right and why.

This chapter was originally published on the author's web site in November 2016.

LIST OF ORGANIZATIONS AND ADVOCACY GROUPS THAT NEED OUR SUPPORT

1. **American Civil Liberties Union:** works to defend individual rights and liberties guaranteed by the Constitution.

2. **Anti-Defamation League:** was founded in 1913 to "stop the defamation of the Jewish people and to secure justice and fair treatment to all. Today, it fights against anti-Semitism and bigotry as one of the largest civil rights organizations in the country.

3. **Asylum Seeker Advocacy Project of the Urban Justice Center:** ASAP works to end the wrongful detention and deportation of refugee women and children in the United States. ASAP amplifies the traditional legal services model through creative use of technology, an international network of engaged volunteers, and innovative approaches to community building and partnership.

4. **Black Lives Matter:** Black Lives Matter is a chapter-based national organization working for the validity of Black life. We are working to (re)build the Black liberation movement.

5. **Border Angels:** is an all-volunteer non-profit that advocates for immigration reform and social justice focusing on the U.S.-Mexico border. It offers educational and awareness programs and migrant outreach programs to San Diego County's immigrant population.

6. **Boys & Girls Clubs of America:** offers enrichment programs and support for children when they're not in school.

7. **Campaign Zero:** advocates for policy solutions to end police violence in America.

8. **Center for Constitutional Rights**: CCR is dedicated to advancing and protecting the rights guaranteed by the United States Constitution and the Universal Declaration of Human Rights. CCR is committed to the creative use of law as a positive force for social change. We do that by combining cutting-edge litigation, advocacy and strategic communications in work on a broad range of civil and human rights issues.

9. **Center for Reproductive Rights:** The Center for Reproductive Rights uses "the law to advance reproductive freedom as a fundamental human right that all governments are legally obligated to protect, respect, and fulfill."

10. **Children and Nature:** The Children & Nature Network is leading the movement to connect all children, their families and communities to nature through innovative ideas, evidence-based resources and tools, broad-based collaboration and support of grassroots leadership.

11. **Climate Science Legal Defense Fund:** The Climate Science Legal Defense Fund (CSLDF) works to defend climate scientists who are dragged into litigation or otherwise threatened with legal attacks and harassment by politically

and ideologically motivated groups.

12. **Council on American-Islamic Relations (CAIR):** is the country's largest Muslim civil liberties organization.

13. **Council on American-Islamic Relations:** CAIR protects the civil rights of all Americans regardless of faith and has served more than 25,000 victims of discrimination since its founding in 1994.

14. **Define American:** Define American is a non-profit media and culture organization that uses the power of story to transcend politics and shift the conversation about immigrants, identity, and citizenship in a changing America.

15. **Design for Progress by Sight Unseen:** Sight Unseen is an online magazine dedicated to the visual arts, but here they've bundled together a group of fantastic charities, all listed here. Through Sight Unseen you can donate simultaneously to Planned Parenthood, Everytown for Gun Safety, the ACLU, the Southern Poverty Law Center, Human Rights Campaign, EarthJustice, and the National Immigration Law Center.

16. **EarthJustice:** is the largest nonprofit environmental law organization in the country, working to protect wildlife, for healthy communities, and for cleaner energy options. The organization represents its clients free of charge.

17. **Ella Baker Center for Human Rights:** Builds the power of black, brown, and poor people to break the cycles of incarceration and poverty and make our communities safe, healthy, and strong.

18. **Emerge America:** Emerge gives Democratic women who want to run for public office a unique opportunity. We are

the only in-depth, seven-month, 70-hour, training program providing aspiring female leaders with cutting-edge tools and training to run for elected office and elevate themselves in our political system.

19. **EMILY's List:** is a political action committee that works to elect pro-choice Democratic women candidates to public office.

20. **Equal Justice Initiative:** The EJI is committed to ending mass incarceration and excessive punishment in the United States, to challenging racial and economic injustice, and to protecting basic human rights for the most vulnerable people in American society.

21. **Esperanza LA:** Esperanza Immigrant Rights Project is a public interest legal organization serving some of the most vulnerable immigrants in the Los Angeles area.

22. **Everytown for Gun Safety:** Everytown for Gun Safety is a movement of Americans fighting for common-sense reforms to reduce gun violence.

23. **GLAAD:** GLAAD works with the media to bring people powerful stories from the LGBT community that build support for equality.

24. **Global Greengrants Fund:** Global Greengrants is the leading environmental fund that supports grassroots action on a global scale." The organization gives "people, foundations, and responsible businesses the opportunity to invest in global grassroots change that honors people, livelihoods, and ecosystems equally.

25. **Hands Up United:** HandsUpUnited is a collective of politically engaged minds building towards the liberation of

oppressed Black, Brown and poor people through education, art, civil disobedience, advocacy and agriculture.

26. **Human Rights Campaign:** The HRC is the largest national lesbian, gay, bisexual, transgender and queer civil rights organization.

27. **Human Rights First:** Human Rights First is a non-profit, nonpartisan international human rights organization based in New York, Washington D.C. and Houston.

28. **Human Rights Watch:** Human Rights Watch researchers work "to expose tyranny, to empower victims, and to tell their stories to the world."

29. **Humanitarian Law Project:** The Humanitarian Law Project is a non-profit organization founded in 1985, dedicated to protecting human rights and promoting the peaceful resolution of conflict by using established international human rights laws and humanitarian law.

30. **Immigrant Defense Project:** Among other things, the Immigrant Defense Project attempts to impact litigation and provides legal advice, advocacy, and post-conviction relief for immigrants.

31. **Immigration Equality:** The nation's leading LGBTQ immigrant rights organization.

32. **Innocence Project:** The Innocence Project exonerates the wrongly convicted through DNA testing and reforms the criminal justice system to prevent future injustice.

33. **International Justice Mission:** A global organization that protects the poor from violence in the developing world. Their global team includes more than 750 lawyers, inves-

tigators, social workers, community activists and other professionals at work through 17 field offices.

34. **Jewish Voice for Peace:** Jewish Voice for Peace members are inspired by Jewish tradition to work together for peace, social justice, equality, human rights, respect for international law, and a U.S. foreign policy based on these ideals.

35. **Kids in Need of Defense:** KIND represents unaccompanied immigrant and refugee children in their deportation proceedings.

36. **Lambda Legal:** Lambda Legal is a national organization committed to achieving full recognition of the civil rights of lesbians, gay men, bisexuals, transgender people and those with HIV through impact litigation, education and public policy work.

37. **Lawyers' Committee for Civil Rights Under Law:**

38. **Legal Aid Foundation of Los Angeles:** Legal Aid Foundation of Los Angeles provides "civil legal aid to poor and low-income people in Los Angeles County."

39. **Legal Aid Society:** The Legal Aid Society is a private, not-for-profit legal services organization, the oldest and largest in the nation, dedicated since 1876 to providing quality legal representation to low-income New Yorkers.

40. **Mazzoni Center:** offers healthcare services to LGBTQ population in Philadelphia, including trans clinical care services, walk-in HIV and STI testing, primary care, and addiction and recovery services.

41. **Meiklejohn Civil Liberties Institute (MCLI):** MCLI is part of the infrastructure of the peace and justice community,

empowering people to protect and expand their rights under law. Meiklejohn is a center for peace law, an organizer for the right to education, an information clearinghouse on social change, an advocate of government accountability, a training center, and repository of history

42. **MPower Change:** MPower Change is a grassroots movement rooted in diverse Muslim communities throughout the United States who are working together to build social, spiritual, racial, and economic justice for all people.

43. **NAACP:** The mission of the NAACP is to ensure the political, educational, social, and economic equality of rights of all persons and to eliminate race-based discrimination.

44. **NAACP Legal Defense Fund:** The NAACP legal defense fund fights for racial justice through litigation, advocacy, and public education.

45. **NARAL Pro-Choice America:** is a political advocacy group focused on fighting for women's reproductive rights and freedom.

46. **National Abortion Federation:** The mission of the National Abortion Federation is to ensure safe, legal, and accessible abortion care, which promotes health and justice for women. Our work supports these three fundamental aspects of our mission: Safe, Legal, and Accessible.

47. **National Coalition Against Domestic Violence (NCADV):** advocates for victims and attempts to change policy surrounding domestic violence.

48. **National Immigration Forum:** is a leading immigrant advocacy group that offers various programs to integrate immigrants into the workforce and obtain citizenship.

49. **National Immigration Law Center:** is dedicated to fighting for the rights of low-income immigrants through litigation, policy analysis and advocacy, and various other methods.

50. **National Network of Abortion Funds:** The National Network of Abortion Funds builds power with members to remove financial and logistical barriers to abortion access by centering people who have abortions and organizing at the intersections of racial, economic, and reproductive justice.

51. **National Organization for Women (NOW):** is an activist organization, foundation and PAC that advocates for equal rights for women. Donate and look for volunteer programs, like clinic escorting, on your local chapter's page.

52. **National Women's Law Center:** The Center has worked for more than 40 years to protect and promote equality and opportunity for women and families. We champion policies and laws that help women and girls achieve their potential at every stage of their lives – at school, at work, at home, and in retirement. Our staff are committed advocates who take on the toughest challenges, especially for the most vulnerable women.

53. **National Youth Rights Association (NYRA):** NYRA is the nation's premier youth rights organization. NYRA is a youth-led national non-profit dedicated to fighting for the civil rights and liberties of young people.

54. **Native American Rights Fund (NARF):** Throughout its history, NARF has impacted tens of thousands of Indian people in its work for more than 250 tribes. Some examples of the results include: protecting and establishing the inherent sovereignty of tribes; obtaining official tribal recognition for numerous Indian tribes; helping tribes continue their

ancient traditions, by protecting their rights to hunt, fish and use the water on their lands; helping to uphold Native American religious freedom; assuring the return of remains and burial goods from museums and historical societies for proper and dignified re-burial; and protecting voting rights of Native Americans

55. **Natural Resources Defense Council (NRDC):** The NRDC works to ensure the rights of all people to the air, the water and the wild, and to prevent special interests from undermining public interests. NRDC experts use data and science to unearth the root causes of the planet's problems.

56. **New York City Alliance Against Sexual Assault:** The mission of the New York City Alliance Against Sexual Assault is to prevent sexual violence and reduce the harm it causes through education, research and advocacy.

57. **NextGen Climate:** works politically to prevent climate disaster.

58. **Our Children's Trust**: Our Children's Trust elevates the voice of youth to secure the legal right to a stable climate and healthy atmosphere for the benefit of all present and future generations.

59. **PEN America:** PEN America stands at the intersection of literature and human rights to protect open expression in the United States and worldwide. They champion the freedom to write, recognizing the power of the word to transform the world. Their mission is to unite writers and their allies to celebrate creative expression and defend the liberties that make it possible.

60. **PFLAG:** PFLAG is the nation's largest family and ally organization dedicated to the LGBT community.

61. **Planned Parenthood:** is the country's leading sexual and reproductive healthcare provider. Donate, and look for nationwide volunteer opportunities, including as a clinic escort.

62. **ProPublica:** Donating to ProPublica supports its independent, non-profit newsroom that produces investigative journalism in the public interest.

63. **Rape, Abuse & Incest National Network (RAINN):** is the country's largest anti-sexual violence organization, which operates the National Sexual Assault Hotline and programs to help victims of sexual violence.

64. **Reproductive Health Access Project:** is a non-profit that trains clinicians to make quality reproductive healthcare more accessible.

65. **Running Start:** is an organization dedicated to educating young women and girls about the importance of politics, through the Young Women's Political Leadership Program and various other fellowships and internships.

66. **Safe Passage Project:** Safe Passage Project addresses the unmet needs of immigrant children living in New York by providing legal representation to empower each child to pursue a safe, stable future.

67. **Sanctuary for Families:** Sanctuary for Families is New York's leading service provider and advocate for survivors of domestic violence, sex trafficking and related forms of gender violence.

68. **She Should Run:** is a non-profit that aims to get more women into elected leadership roles.

69. **Sierra Club**: is the largest grassroots environmental organization in the county, and works to protect millions of acres of wilderness and pass legislation like the Clean Air Act and the Clean Water Act.

70. **Society of Professional Journalists Legal Defense Fund:** The Society of Professional Journalists collects and distributes contributions for aiding journalists in defending the freedom of speech and press guaranteed by the First Amendment of the United States Constitution.

71. **Southern Poverty Law Center (SPLC):** fights hate groups and bigotry using education, litigation, and advocacy.

72. **Sylvia Rivera Law Project:** provides legal services specifically to low-income people and people of color who are transgender, intersex, or gender non-conforming.

73. **The New York Immigration Coalition:** The New York Immigration Coalition aims to achieve a fairer and more just society that values the contributions of immigrants and extends opportunity to all. The NYIC promotes immigrants' full civic participation, fosters their leadership, and provides a unified voice and a vehicle for collective action for New York's diverse immigrant communities.

74. **The Dream US:** TheDream.US is a new multimillion dollar National Scholarship Fund for DREAMers, created to help immigrant youth who've received DACA achieve their American Dream through the completion of a college education.

75. **Trans Lifeline:** The Trans Lifeline is a hotline staffed by transgender people for transgender people.

76. **Trevor Project:** The Trevor Project is the leading national

organization providing crisis intervention and suicide prevention services to lesbian, gay, bisexual, transgender and questioning (LGBTQ) young people ages 13-24.

77. **Union of Concerned Scientists:** Our scientists and engineers develop and implement innovative, practical solutions to some of our planet's most pressing problems – from combating global warming and developing sustainable ways to feed, power, and transport ourselves, to fighting misinformation, advancing racial equity, and reducing the threat of nuclear war.

78. **Urgent Action Fund for Women's Human Rights:** Urgent Action Fund for Women's Human Rights is a global women's fund that protects, strengthens and sustains women and transgender human rights defenders at critical moments.

79. **US Human Rights Network:** The US Human Rights Network is a national network of organizations and individuals working to build and strengthen a people-centered human rights movement in the United States, where leadership is centered on those most directly affected by human rights violations, and the full range of diversity within communities is respected and embraced.

80. **Women Organized Against Rape:** Women Organized Against Rape is a non-profit organization whose mission is to eliminate sexual violence through specialized treatment services, comprehensive prevention education programs, and advocacy for the rights of survivors of sexual assault. WOAR provides free counseling for women, men, and children who have experienced sexual violence.

81. **Workplace Fairness:** Workplace Fairness believes that fair treatment of workers is sound public policy and good

business practice, and that free access to comprehensive, unbiased information about workers' rights - without legal jargon - is an essential ingredient in any fair workplace.

82. **Young Center for Immigrant Children's Rights**: works to protect the best interests of children who come to the U.S. on their own.

REFERENCES

The Principles For Which We Fight

1. *Civitas: A Framework for Civic Education, a Collaborative Project of the Center for Civic Education and the Council for the Advancement of Citizenship*, National Council for the Social Studies Bulletin No. 86, 1991.

Love Trumps Hate

2. https://www.splcenter.org/hatewatch/2016/11/11/over-200-incidents-hateful-harassment-andintimidation-election-day

3. http://www.qotd.org/search/single.html?qid=70865

4. http://www.qotd.org/search/single.html?qid=70866

5. https://www.ft.com/content/eb87a71a-a7f9-11e6-8898-79a99e2a4de6

I'm A Scientist. This Is What I'll Fight For

6. https://the-macroscope.org/the-war-on-facts-is-a-war-on-democracy-5f565c28a385#.82ogwqlzg

7. https://www.marchforscience.com

On Donald Trump, Nelson Mandela, Racism And Making Friends With Your Enemies

8. http://www.nytimes.com/1985/08/16/opinion/l-yesterday-s-nazi-sympathizers-today-s-south-african-leaders-195124.html

9. http://www.history.com/news/history-lists/5-attacks-on-u-s-soil-during-world-war-ii

10. http://mg.co.za/article/2014-05-01-the-lesson-the-murder-of-david-webster-holds-for-thepresent

11. https://www.nobelprize.org/nobel_prizes/peace/laureates/1984/tutu-facts.html

12. https://www.washingtonpost.com/archive/politics/1990/03/08/south-african-assassin-describes-death-squads/7a3c9f51-f87c-4400-97f6-8e4d7bb06b60/?utm_term=.2b634ef79516

13. https://www.ushmm.org/wlc/en/article.php?ModuleId=10007392

14. https://www.youtube.com/watch?v=kgcXWfRtIds

15. http://www.cnn.com/2008/WORLD/africa/07/01/mandela.watch/

Zombie Politics And All The Big Lies Reborn In Trumplandia

16. https://radicalscholarship.wordpress.com/2016/02/19/investigating-zombies-to-foster-genre-awareness/

17. https://theconversation.com/pride-prejudice-and-the-mutation-of-zombies-from-caribbeanslaves-to-flesh-eaters-54996

18. http://nepc.colorado.edu/blog/shifting-talking-points-among-school-choice-advocates

19. https://www.washingtonpost.com/news/the-fix/wp/2016/11/16/post-truth-named-2016-word-of-the-year-by-oxford-dictionaries/

20. https://beta.theglobeandmail.com/opinion/the-fake-war-on-fake-news/article33347119/

21. http://www.truthdig.com/report/item/fake_news_homegrown_and_far_from_new_20161218

22. https://radicalscholarship.wordpress.com/2014/06/19/u-s-and-education-reform-need-a-critical-free-press/

23. http://www.theonion.com/article/woman-a-leading-authority-on-what-shouldnt-be-in-p-35922

24. https://www.nytimes.com/2017/01/18/us/fake-news-hillary-clinton-cameron-harris.html

25. https://www.washingtonpost.com/news/answer-sheet/wp/2013/10/28/five-stereotypes-about-poor-families-and-education/?utm_term=.f9a67242c393

26. https://www.nytimes.com/2015/06/01/world/americas/ex-fifa-official-jack-warner-citesonion-article-in-defense.html

27. https://radicalscholarship.wordpress.com/2017/01/05/you-dont-know-nothing-u-s-has-always-shunned-the-expert/

28. https://www.nytimes.com/2017/01/13/well/eat/food-stamp-snap-soda.html?_r=0

29. http://kdvr.com/2017/01/15/tennessee-could-ban-people-from-using-food-stamps-to-buy-soda-ice-cream-other-junk-food/

30. http://www.sheilabutt.com/rep-sheila-butt-its-time-for-food-stamp-reform/

31. http://www.sheilabutt.com/

32. http://www.tennessean.com/story/news/politics/2017/01/13/columbia-lawmaker-files-billprohibit-unhealthy-foods-foodstamps/96545368/?hootPostID=cc9951c13c2afd17ed37077c53f19d1a

33. https://www.jacobinmag.com/2017/01/food-stamps-snap-welfare-soda-new-york-times/

34. https://www.nytimes.com/2017/01/13/well/eat/food-stamp-snap-soda.html

35. https://www.fns.usda.gov/sites/default/files/ops/SNAPFoodsTypicallyPurchased.pdf

36. https://opinionator.blogs.nytimes.com/2013/11/02/poverty-in-america-is-mainstream/

37. https://obamawhitehouse.archives.gov/administration/eop/cea/economic-report-of-the-President/2014

38. https://radicalscholarship.wordpress.com/2016/05/03/how-good-is-the-best-edujournalism/

39. https://radicalscholarship.wordpress.com/2014/06/19/u-s-and-education-reform-need-a-critical-free-press/

40. https://radicalscholarship.wordpress.com/2017/01/14/from-sports-fanaticism-to-plagiarism-this-week-in-what-is-wrong-with-education/

41. https://radicalscholarship.wordpress.com/2014/06/19/u-s-and-education-reform-need-a-critical-free-press/

42. https://radicalscholarship.wordpress.com/2015/01/17/liberal-hollywood-a-reader/

43. https://www.amazon.com/Cats-Cradle-Novel-Kurt-Vonnegut/dp/038533348X/

44. https://radicalscholarship.wordpress.com/2014/10/31/the-delusion-of-choice/

45. https://radicalscholarship.wordpress.com/2016/10/27/republicans-have-a-yuge-logic-problem/

46. http://www.thekingcenter.org/archive/document/mlk-republican-nomination-barry-goldwater

47. http://www.huffingtonpost.com/entry/this-mlk-quote-sums-up-the-

rise-of-white-supremacypost-trump_us_5875426de4b099cdb1000431

48. http://www.huffingtonpost.com/entry/malcolm-x-predicted-how-black-people-would-feelunder-a-trump-presidency_us_582496fce4b07751c390cae9

49. http://www.edweek.org/ew/projects/the-leftward-tilt-of-education-scholarship.html

50. http://www.edweek.org/ew/articles/2017/01/11/ideological-diversity-is-the-price-of-edscholars.html

51. http://digitalcommons.buffalostate.edu/jiae/vol4/iss1/4/#.U48xfAblJ7I.wordpress

52. https://radicalscholarship.wordpress.com/2016/12/01/i-too-am-a-dangerous-professor-if-you-covet-ignorance-hatred/

53. http://www.crmvet.org/info/bhammean.htm

54. https://www.amazon.com/Dog-Whistle-Politics-Appeals-Reinvented/dp/019022925X

The Red Queen

55. https://www.scribd.com/doc/313106623/Michigan-Achieves-2016-Michigan-State-of-Education-Report

56. https://www.mackinac.org/2041

57. http://www.csmonitor.com/1993/1008/08031.html

58. http://www.mlive.com/politics/index.ssf/2013/12/snyder_contributions_issue_ads.html

59. http://www.metrotimes.com/detroit/once-again-michigan-dems-receive-more-votes-in-thestate-house-but-republicans-hold-onto-power/Content?oid=2472685

60. http://www.freep.com/story/news/politics/2015/11/09/michigan-ranks-last-laws-ethicstransparency/75288210/

61. https://www.surveymonkey.com/r/2016_glep

62. http://www.freep.com/story/news/politics/2016/08/12/grand-traverse-gop-disowns-ex-govmilliken-over-his-clinton-support/88641468/

63. http://www.mlive.com/lansing-news/index.ssf/2016/01/gov_rick_snyder_signs_campaign.html

64. http://www.mlive.com/news/index.ssf/2016/07/federal_judge_stops_michigan_l.html

65. http://www.detroitnews.com/story/news/education/2015/08/16/mich-

igan-enrollment/31834901/

66. http://www.mlive.com/lansing-news/index.ssf/2015/07/gov_snyder_signs_early_financi.html

67. http://abcnews.go.com/Politics/michigan-governor-signs-work-bill-law/story?id=17934332

68. http://www.freep.com/story/news/politics/2016/02/05/judge-puts-michigan-gag-orderelection-law-hold/79888702/

69. http://mcfn.org/node/6043/devos-family-made-14-million-in-political-contributions-in-thelast-2-years-alone

70. http://www.freep.com/story/news/politics/2016/02/02/bills-move-punish-teachers-districtssick-outs/79689772/

71. http://woodtv.com/2016/01/07/detroit-schools-chief-knocks-teachers-over-sickouts/

72. http://www.cnn.com/2016/05/02/us/detroit-schools-teacher-sickout/

73. http://www.metrotimes.com/detroit/the-eaa-exposed-an-investigativereport/Content?oid=2249513

74. http://edushyster.com/long-game-of-betsy-devos/

How Big Data Becomes Psy Ops And Tilts The World Towards Its Own Aims: Next Stop, Public Education

75. http://motherboard.vice.com/en_us/article/big-data-cambridge-analytica-brexit-trump

76. https://sclgroup.cc/elections

77. https://cambridgeanalytica.org/about

78. Cadwalladr, C. (2016). Google, democracy and the truth about internet search. The Guardian. https://www.theguardian.com/technology/2016/dec/04/google-democracy-truth-internet-search-facebook

79. http://www.independent.co.uk/news/world/americas/cambridge-analytica-steve-bannonrobert-rebekah-mercer-donald-trump-conflicts-of-interest-white-a7435536.html

80. Cattell, R. B. (1957). *Personality and motivation: Structure and measurement.* New York, NY: World Book.

81. http://faculty.ferris.edu/ISAR/bios/Cattell/genetica.htm

82. http://fairtest.org/racism-eugenics-and-testing-again

83. http://www.ets.org/s/successnavigator/pdf/learning_abstracts_markle_obanion.pdf

84. MacCann, C., Duckworth, A.L., & Roberts. R.D. (2009). Empirical identification of the major facets of *Conscientiousness*. *Learning and Individual Differences*, 19, 451–458. http://www.sas.upenn.edu/~duckwort/images/Conscientiousness2009.pdf

85. https://radicalscholarship.wordpress.com/2014/12/04/grit-education-narratives-veneer-for-white-wealth-privilege

86. U.S. Dept of Education, Office of Technology "Promoting Grit, Tenacity, and Perseverance: Critical Factors for Success in the 21st Century" (2013). Retrieved from: http://www.pgbovine.net/OET-Draft-Grit-Report-2-17-13.pdf

87. http://www.youtube.com/watch?v=nka-_Mhp7f0

88. http://www.youtube.com/watch?v=0qmrngbjFWg

89. http://artforum.com/diary/id=56948

90. http://www.privacylab.at/wp-content/uploads/2016/09/Christl-Networks__K_o.pdf

91. http://www.pearsoned.com/wp-content/uploads/Cite2016ProgramGuide_singlepages_FINAL_nocrops.pdf

92. http://www.pearsoned.com/events-and-webinars/cite/program/pre-conference-sessions/

93. http://www.pearsoned.com/wp-content/uploads/Cite2016_MeasuringLearningImpact_Tuesday_1-150PM.pdf

94. Klein, N. (2014). *This Changes Everything: The Climate vs. Capitalism.* New York, NY: Simon and Schuster

Trump Says Our Schools Are "Flush with Cash!?" They're Falling Apart!

95. https://www.yahoo.com/news/read-donald-trump-full-inaugural-172850356.html

96. http://articles.latimes.com/2013/mar/12/local/la-me-0313-lopez-dis-repair-20130313

97. http://www.seiu32bj.org/falling-further-apart-decaying-schools-in-new-york-citys-poorest-neighborhoods/

98. https://www.nytimes.com/2016/01/21/us/crumbling-destitute-schools-threaten-detroitsrecovery.html

99. http://blogs.edweek.org/edweek/campaign-k-12/2017/01/trump_american_schools_flush_w.html

100. https://gadflyonthewallblog.wordpress.com/2015/07/09/do-americans-

throw-money-at-their-schools-a-fair-funding-primer/

101. http://www.pbs.org/newshour/updates/education-july-dec96-school_funding_10-03/

102. http://www.ascd.org/publications/educational-leadership/may02/vol59/num08/Unequal-School-Funding-in-the-United-States.aspx

103. http://www.lincolninst.edu/publications/policy-focus-reports/property-tax-school-funding-dilemma

104. http://www.ascd.org/publications/educational-leadership/may02/vol59/num08/Unequal-School-Funding-in-the-United-States.aspx

105. http://blogs.edweek.org/edweek/campaign-k-12/2017/01/trump_american_schools_flush_w.html

106. https://dianeravitch.net/2013/12/03/my-view-of-the-pisa-scores/

107. https://www.mitchellrobinson.net/2015/06/13/the-one-about-data-numbers-and-truth/

108. https://www.nap.edu/read/12521/chapter/1

109. https://news.wsu.edu/

110. http://portside.org/2015-01-22/more-half-us-public-school-students-live-poverty-report-finds

111. http://www.jstor.org/stable/30192587?seq=1#page_scan_tab_contents

112. https://gadflyonthewallblog.wordpress.com/2017/01/10/self-serving-public-servants-trump-devos-and-the-rise-of-the-plutocrats/

The Racist Genie Is Out Of The Bottle (Again): A Student-Teacher Discussion

113. http://www.nytimes.com/2016/11/11/opinion/denounce-the-hate-mr-trump.html

Empathy, Diversity, And Being "Mean To All People": The Democratic Work Of The Public's Schools In Hard Times

114. Hochschild, A. (2016). *Strangers in their own land: Anger and mourning on the American right.* New York: The New Press.

115. Bazelon, E. (2016, November 16). Bullying in the age of Trump. *New York Times.* Retrieved from https://www.nytimes.com/2016/11/16/opinion/bullying-in-the-age-of-trump.html?_r=0

116. Costello, M.B. (2016). *The Trump effect: The impact of the presidential campaign on our nation's schools.* Montgomery: Southern Poverty Law

Center. Retrieved from https://www.splcenter.org/20160413/trump-effect-impact-presidential-campaign-our-nations-schools

117. Roth-Hanania, R., Davidov, M., & Zahn-Waxler, C. (2011). Empathy development from 8 to 16 months: Early signs of concern for others. *Infant Behavior and Development, 34*, 447-458.

118. Coates, T. (2015). *Between the world and me.* New York: Spiegel and Grau.

119. Osario, S. (in preparation). No room for silence: The impact of the 2016 presidential candidate race on a second-grade dual-language (Spanish-English) classroom.

120. Baltodano, M. (2012). Neoliberalism and the demise of public education: the corporatization of schools of education. *International Journal of Qualitative Studies in Education, 25*, 487-507.

121. Nussbaum, M. (2016). *Not for profit: Why democracy needs the humanities*, new paperback edition with new preface. Princeton: Princeton University Press.

122. Genishi, C., & Dyson, A. Haas. (2009). *Children, language, and literacy: Diverse learners in diverse times.* New York and Washington, DC: Teachers College Press & The National Association for the Education of Young Children.

123. Volk, D. (2017). Join us in a 'space of dialogue and human action.' *Early Years, 37*, 1-16. http://dx.doi.org/10.1080/09575146.2016.1272926

124. Dyson, A. Haas. (2015). The search for inclusion: Deficit discourse and the erasure of childhoods. *Language Arts, 92*, 199-207

125. Dewey, J. (1916). *Democracy and education.* New York: The Free Press

126. Greene, M. (1988). *The dialectic of freedom.* New York: Teachers College Press.

Peacemaking And The Search For Home In Dark Times

127. Fine, E.S. (2015). *Raising Peacemakers.* New York: Garn Press

128. https://www.youtube.com/watch?v=iMtXTJ0lELY

129. http://www.childrenaspeacemakers.ca/

130. http://www.artasiapacific.com/Magazine/81/SetAdriftAlfredoAndIsabelAquilizan

www.ingramcontent.com/pod-product-compliance
Lightning Source LLC
Chambersburg PA
CBHW051729020426
42333CB00014B/1219